The Vision of Catholic Youth Ministry
Fundamentals, Theory, and Practice

D1417298

Robert J. McCarty, DMin, General Editor

with

Laurie Delgatto, Rev. Tom Dunne, SDB, Michelle Hernandez, Jeffrey Kaster, Leif Kehrwald, Maggie McCarty, Frank Mercadante, Greg "Dobie" Moser, Barbara A. Murray, Randy Raus, Sean Reynolds, Tony Tamberino, Terri Telepak, and Anne-Marie Yu-Phelps

saint mary's press

The publishing team included Laurie Delgatto, development editor; Lorraine Kilmartin, reviewer; Mary Koehler, permissions editor; prepress and manufacturing coordinated by the prepublications and production services departments of Saint Mary's Press.

Printed in the United States of America

3310

ISBN 978-0-88489-836-8

Library of Congress Cataloging-in-Publication Data

The vision of Catholic youth ministry : fundamentals, theory, and practice / Robert J. McCarty, general editor with Laurie Delgatto . . . [et al.].
    p. cm.
ISBN 0-88489-836-9 (pbk.)
    1. Church work with youth—Catholic Church. I. McCarty, Robert J. II. Delgatto, Laurie.
BX2347.8.Y7V48 2005
259'.23'088282—dc22

                             2004027672

With admiration and appreciation for my colleagues who are passionate about the practice and profession of Catholic youth ministry and through whose efforts we now have comprehensive ministry formation and competency-based standards for the field, . . . and with gratitude for those Catholic youth ministry leaders whose commitment to the young Church spurs them to pursue professional ministerial development.

Contents

Introduction

This textbook is long overdue! The practice and profession of Catholic youth ministry has grown significantly, as evidenced by the increased number of youth ministry coordinators in parishes, campus ministry coordinators in schools, and independent ministry providers serving parishes and dioceses. Likewise the range of responsibilities assigned to diocesan offices of youth ministry has expanded to include consultations and direct services, leadership development and certification processes, pastoral care and crisis response, adolescent catechesis, and training for youth protection and safe environments. Some dioceses have combined youth ministry, college-campus ministry, and young-adult ministry into a single office. However, while providing more effective coordination of ministry, expanding responsibilities often do not include increased staff and budget resources.

The context for youth ministry has also changed. Increasingly, youth ministry encompasses young people from early adolescence through early young adulthood. Further, a significant and intentional ministry to young people is now found in cultural and ethnic communities. The family and social contexts of young people have also become important emphases in ministry.

A Historical Context

An interesting piece of youth ministry trivia is identifying the first organized program for Catholic young people. In 1930 Bishop Bernard J. Sheil, in Chicago, launched the Catholic Youth Organization (CYO) with his boxing program, responding to the need for youth to have alternatives to hanging out on the streets. The original CYO charter describes its purpose in this way: "To promote among Catholic youth a recreational, educational, and religious program that will adequately meet their physical, mental, and spiritual needs in their after school hours . . . while instilling in their minds and hearts a true love of God and country" (*Hope for the Decade,* p. 4). Organized ministry with young people had arrived.

For the past thirty-some years, and perhaps since Vatican II and its vision of Church and ministry gave impetus to the explosion in lay ministry, a vision for youth ministry has been unfolding in the Catholic Church. Its roots are in the Catholic youth work of the 1950s and 1960s, best exemplified by the Catholic Youth Organization and its five components of religious, athletic, cultural, social, and service activities; and the Confraternity for Christian Doctrine, which was responsible for the religious education of Catholic youth in public schools, in the Catholic school system, and in myriad youth movements and programs such as the Young Catholic Students, Catholic scouting, Sodality, Columbian Squires, and other youth organizations.

During the 1960s and 1970s, other expressions of youth ministry were instituted, including Teens Encounter Christ (TEC), SEARCH, other similar retreat programs, and the Knights of Saint Peter Claver. Cultural and ethnic communities; urban, suburban, and rural communities; and various sections of the country all developed approaches to youth ministry specific to the needs and gifts of their young people.

In 1972 the United States Conference of Catholic Bishops (USCCB), then known as the United States Catholic Conference (USCC), published the document *The Diocesan Youth Director* to "assist youth directors in clarifying objectives and to help them determine specific programs for youth in their dioceses." The same document states:

> [There is] a need for a total program for youth's leisure hours . . . to enable youth to engage in the work of the Church in the world; to bring a specific focus to the work of religious education, namely education for mission . . . by creating and supporting programs and projects that provide an opportunity for youth to engage in activities that exemplify what it means to be Christian in the world today; to interpret youth and advocate their concerns; to provide services that answer the real needs of youth. (From *Hope for the Decade*, p. 2)

This was the first in a series of national documents that developed a unified vision of youth ministry.

In 1975 the USCC advisory board for youth activities commissioned a paper on total youth ministry as an in-depth study of the field. Published in 1976, *A Vision of Youth Ministry* identified dimensions, components, and principles of the multifaceted nature of youth ministry. Providing this shared vision was a significant contribution to the field of youth ministry.

Throughout the 1970s and early 1980s, youth ministry became an established reality at various levels: dioceses opened youth ministry offices or changed the name of existing offices to reflect a growing understanding of youth ministry, the first parish youth ministry coordinators were hired, colleges offered workshops and courses, and training programs for youth and adults were developed. Building on *A Vision of Youth Ministry,* the Church's approach became more comprehensive, and the field and practice of youth ministry became more professional.

In 1982 the National Federation for Catholic Youth Ministry (NFCYM) was established, creating a network for diocesan offices and providing resources, leadership, and vision for the ministry. A series of documents on adolescent catechesis, evangelization, and liturgy and prayer, written in consultation with practitioners in youth ministry, further clarified various dimensions of the ministry. The role of the coordinator of youth ministry was also solidified as a ministry career through the development of competency-based standards by the NFCYM, first published in 1991 and revised in 2003. The standards identify the knowledge and skills integral to the profession and professionalism of youth ministry leaders. The competency-based standards also provide a framework for the development of systematic adult training and certification models.

The decade of the nineties was characterized by an expanding understanding of youth ministry. Evangelization, social justice, and pastoral care were more fully integrated into the ministry. Various youth movements continued to develop. Organizations such as the National African American Catholic Youth Ministry Network and the National Catholic Network Pastoral Juvenil Hispana focused on cultural and ethnic communities. Training and leadership development programs for youth and for adults were well established. And Catholic publishers developed practical resources and catechetical materials to support the ministry.

Of particular note, in August 1993 Pope John Paul II and World Youth Day came to Denver, and national attention was directed toward the young Catholic Church by both the secular press and

Church authorities. The quiet but steady growth of youth ministry now gained public prominence.

The 1997 document *Renewing the Vision: A Framework for Catholic Youth Ministry* signaled an important era in ministry. Whereas the original *Vision of Youth Ministry* document was published by a department at the USCC, *Renewing the Vision* was a mandate of the entire National Conference of Catholic Bishops and confirmed what had been happening throughout the field of youth ministry. The ministry now called upon the entire Church community to see themselves as ministers to young people. Youth are called to responsible participation in the pastoral and liturgical life of the faith community. Perhaps one of the most significant shifts in youth ministry in the past decade is the attention to families as the primary context for young people, and therefore an important dimension of comprehensive youth ministry. The family, the parish, and the larger social community are now the arena for ministry to young people. And dioceses and colleges recognize the need and desire for systematic formation and academic credentialing for the profession of the Catholic youth ministry leader.

The Vision of Catholic Youth Ministry: Fundamentals, Theory, and Practice

The need for this textbook reflects the growth in the profession and practice of Catholic youth ministry. With the growth of diocesan ministry formation programs and college degree and certificate programs, having a foundational text to accompany the core youth ministry documents will provide a common language along with the shared vision.

It is appropriate that this text was written not by a sole author but by a team of competent and passionate practitioners, reflecting the collaborative nature of ministry. The purpose of the text is to provide an introduction to a Catholic understanding and approach to youth ministry, based on *Renewing the Vision* and the *General Directory for Catechesis*. The following chapters describe a theology for youth ministry, break open more fully the goals and components of comprehensive youth ministry, and provide a snapshot of young people today. This textbook also considers the integral dimensions of family and culture in youth ministry, as well as the specific setting of youth ministry in a Catholic school. Further, the inclusion of chapters on youth ministry leadership and organizing for youth ministry provide direction for creating practical structures to assure and support the ministry.

This is an introductory textbook; it is not an encyclopedia of Catholic youth ministry methods and techniques, nor is it designed to be the definitive treatment of components and dimensions. Rather, this textbook provides an overview with pastoral implications and questions to encourage readers to consider practical applications to their ministry setting. Further, a bibliography refers readers to additional resources, which will provide an in-depth understanding of the components and dimensions.

We are challenged to build on the past eighty years of organized Catholic youth ministry. As we create an ever-evolving vision and approach to ministry to, with, by, and for the young Church, we remember the central mission of calling young people to be disciples of Jesus Christ. Welcome to a noble adventure!

Chapter 1

Theology and Catholic Youth Ministry

Rev. Tom Dunne, SDB

Introduction

As the Catholic youth ministry community grows toward its thirtieth year since the publication of *A Vision of Youth Ministry*, in 1976, it is important that those engaged in youth ministry establish the foundations of its mission for its own faithfulness to the Gospel and for those who will carry on this ministry in the years to come.

Objectives

This chapter explores the nature of the relationship between youth ministry and theology, proposes a number of basic theological principles that underlie Catholic youth ministry, and offers some concrete pastoral applications for integrating a theological consciousness into the practice of Catholic youth ministry.

Obstacles to Overcome

To many in the Catholic youth ministry community, the study of theology seems to be irrelevant, theoretical, intimidating, and potentially divisive:

- "There is so much to do in the parish that I don't have the time or energy to study the theological foundations of our ministry."
- "Theology is not practical enough. It doesn't directly relate to my ministry."
- "There are so many areas of study in theology, where would I start? I feel unprepared and overwhelmed."
- "I don't want to get caught up in those divisive theological debates. I only want to proclaim the Good News of Jesus."

Theology and Catholic Youth Ministry

Theology can be defined quite simply in the words of Saint Anselm (d. 1109): "faith seeking understanding." A modern-day theologian offered the following definition:

> Theology may be defined as the study which, through participation in and reflection upon a religious faith, seeks to express the content of this faith in the clearest and most coherent language available. (John Macquarrie, *Principles of Christian Theology,* 2nd ed., p. 1)

Youth ministry must be understood in terms of the mission and ministry of the whole Church, the community of persons who believe in Jesus Christ and continue his saving work through the action of the Holy Spirit. The earlier of the two guiding documents for Catholic youth ministry, *A Vision of Youth Ministry*, offers this basic description:

> The Church's mission is three-fold: to proclaim the good news of salvation; to offer itself as a group of people transformed by the Spirit into a community of faith, hope, and love; and to bring God's justice and love to others through service in its individual, social, and political dimensions. (P. 3)

The document relied on ecclesiology (a theology of the Church) to provide the theological foundation for youth ministry, drawing from the teachings of Vatican II as interpreted, in part, by a contemporary theologian. The writers of the earlier document, *A Vision of Youth Ministry,* relied most heavily on *Dogmatic Constitution on the Church (Lumen Gentium)* and *Pastoral Constitution on the Church in the Modern World (Gaudium et Spes).*

Twenty years later, research demonstrated that *A Vision of Youth Ministry* was effective in promoting the new approach for Catholic youth ministry. The 1996 study of parish youth ministry program participants, *New Directions in Youth Ministry,* found that participation in parish youth ministry programs had a positive effect on both young people and parish life itself (as reported in *Renewing the Vision*, p. 5). The research also demonstrated a close connection between pastoral practice and the understanding of ecclesiology found in *A Vision of Youth Ministry*. However, that document limited its ecclesiology, for the most part, to the local church or parish.

Following up on the encouraging results from their research, the U.S. bishops commissioned a document to give renewed vision and form to the new situation in which the Church and young people found themselves. In defining the foundational assumptions of this updated vision, the writers of *Renewing the Vision* remedied the disconnect between youth ministry and the larger Church. They brought together the teachings of Pope John Paul II, the pastoral experience and reflections of the Catholic youth ministry community, and the pastoral statements of the U.S. bishops.

Renewing the Vision states this new foundational principle of youth ministry in its first and primary goal: "To help young people learn what it means to follow Jesus Christ and to live as disciples today, empowering them to serve others and to work toward a world built on the vision and values of the reign of God" (p. 9). Instead of centering Catholic youth ministry on the local Church community or the youth ministry community, *Renewing the Vision* expands the notion of Church to the entire Catholic faith community. By participating in all aspects of the broader Church life, young people grow in faith "as they experience life in community and actively participate in the mission of Jesus Christ and his Church" (p. 11). In formulating this new vision and framework for Catholic youth ministry, the writers of *Renewing the Vision* define the nature and mission of the Church as centered on God's Reign.

The effect of broadening the theological foundations of Catholic youth ministry is nothing short of radical. The themes of Catholic youth ministry enumerated in *Renewing the Vision* flow out of this changed understanding. By inviting and empowering "young people to live as disciples of Jesus Christ in the world today" (p. 9) through "responsible participation in the life, mission, and work of the Catholic faith community" (p. 11), ministry with the young moves beyond a ministry centered on "my parish" or "my youth group." Instead, *Renewing the Vision* points to a new reality in which Catholic youth ministry takes place in a context that is as broad as the Church itself: family friendly, multicultural, intergenerational, communitywide.

A Vision of Youth Ministry states the theological foundation of ministry within the Christian context: "Because ministry involves the giving of self in relationship to another, the Church's youth ministry must be founded in the radical commitment to lay down one's life in service to the young people whose lives are touched" (p. 4). The document uses the powerful words of Henri Nouwen to describe this ministry of relationship as laying down one's life for another:

> Ministry means the ongoing attempt to put one's own search for God, with all the moments of pain and joy, despair and hope, at the disposal of those who want to join this search but do not know how. . . . We lay down our life to give new life. (P. 111)

> We realize that young people call for Christians who are willing to develop their sensitivity to God's presence in their own lives, as well as the lives of others, and to offer their experience as a way of recognition and liberation to their fellow people. (*Creative Ministry*, p. 116)

By their very lives and the loving service of self-giving they offer to and with the young, youth ministers contribute to the theological reflection of the Catholic community. By their ministry of self-giving and their subsequent reflection on those experiences, youth ministers deepen their own spiritual lives and contribute to the Church's ongoing search for the clearest and most coherent way to express the mysteries of Christian faith.

Theological Principles Underlying Catholic Youth Ministry

Church Defined

Church is the central foundation, giving form to Catholic youth ministry. Therefore, a clear understanding of Church is the essential beginning point for all endeavors in Catholic youth ministry. For the purposes of this chapter, the following working definition of *church*, taken from the *Catechism of the Catholic Church (CCC)*, will serve as an adequate starting point for exploring this foundational concept:

> In Christian usage, the word "church" designates the liturgical assembly, but also the local community, or the whole universal community of believers. These three meanings are inseparable. "The Church" is the People of God that gathers in the whole world. She exists in local communities, and is made real as a liturgical, above all a Eucharistic, assembly. She draws her life from the word and the Body of Christ and so herself becomes Christ's body. (No. 752)

Mission of the Church

The mission of the Church is focused on the Kingdom of God. Its entire existence is directed at offering all people a living witness of God's redemptive presence through the life, death, and Resurrection of Jesus and the power of God's reconciling Spirit. Theologians have described three basic elements of the living Church: *kerygma,* *diakonia,* and *koinonia* (proclamation, service, and community).

First, the Church must be people among whom the Gospel is proclaimed. In proclaiming that the salvation promised by the prophets has come and has become visible in the life, death, and Resurrection of Jesus Christ, the Church challenges all to live a new life of service to God and the world.

The proclamation of the Gospel reveals the second element, which is service. The cross is a call to live for others, just as Christ was and is for others. In service the Church works to bring into reality the justice, peace, and freedom that are essential characteristics of God's Reign.

Finally, the community is the people among whom the Gospel is proclaimed. It is also the assembly among whom service is affirmed, directed, and supported.

Fulfilling the mission of the Church is an ongoing challenge to keep in balance these three elements as we live and worship as God's people. But when this balance occurs, the Church has a remarkable ability to reform lives by building a Gospel-formed and Eucharistic-based community of diverse people who are united in a mutual love of and service to God, one another, and the world.

Rooted in Everyday Experiences

Rooted in the mission of bringing the Lord's compassion for poor and needy people to the young, Catholic youth ministry has approached young people and their experiences as a locus of God's presence. In effect, signs of God's redemptive power are to be found amid and within the most profound levels of everyday life experiences. By reflecting deeply on ordinary life experiences, people of faith encounter traces of the sacred, hidden below the surface, that transform ordinary existence into signs of God's presence.

In 1986 the NFCYM developed a publication on adolescent catechesis, titled *The Challenge of Adolescent Catechesis: Maturing in Faith*, that introduced this principle into the development of Catholic youth ministry in the following way: "Adolescent catechesis encourages young people 'to reflect on their significant experiences and respond to God's presence there'[1]" (p. 9). That perspective gave form to the entire enterprise of adolescent catechesis:

> The fundamental process of adolescent catechesis involves discovering the relationships among the Catholic Christian tradition; God's present activity in the life of the adolescent, family, community, and world; and the contemporary life experience of the adolescent. (P. 9)

In 1993 this principle was a central part in the NFCYM's publication *The Challenge of Catholic Youth Evangelization: Called to Be Witnesses and Storytellers*, which stated:

> The starting point for youth evangelization is our recognition of the presence of God already in young people, their experiences, their families and their culture. . . . Evangelization, therefore, enables young people to uncover and name the experience of a God already active and present in their lives. (P. 7)

This theological principle has been the keystone in the development of Catholic youth ministry's special charism over the past two decades. Its effective presence can be discerned as the foundational understanding underlying most, if not all, Catholic youth ministry resources, processes, and gatherings. As such it remains a treasure of the Catholic community and a prophetic presence to all ministries that come in contact with Catholic youth ministry.

Rooted in Community Life

Catholic youth ministry has always defined itself in terms of building relationships as a way of proclaiming God's word:

> Through witness, outreach, hospitality and a genuine sense of welcome, young people are invited into the Christian community, in which their faith can be nurtured. A community of believers best enables young people to experience deeply the Good News of Christ by nurturing a sense of belonging and acceptance, a sense of "being home" in the parish, in the diocese, and in the universal church. (*The Challenge of Catholic Youth Evangelization,* p. 20)

In the early days of Catholic youth ministry, this perspective on ministry and Christian life was conceived of as promoting and sustaining personal growth and encountering the Lord Jesus through interpersonal relationships. However, in light of the Church's renewed self-understanding, found in more recent Catholic youth ministry literature, the model of community requires transformation to include outreach to a broader community of believers and to all people throughout the world.

Pastoral Applications

Attention to Theological Foundations

An explicit attention to the theological foundations of Catholic youth ministry demands that youth ministry leaders are provided with opportunities to develop greater familiarity with the basic teachings, rites, and ways of living of the Church. It is only with a deeper knowledge of the authentic traditions of the Catholic community that adult leaders will be able to enter fully into the theological reflection that is so essential to their lives as disciples of the Lord, their membership in the Church community, and their active participation in the Church's ministry to and with young people.

Theological Reflection

Catholic Church teaching affirms that ministry, in and of itself, constitutes a way to holiness. Attention to the theological implications of their ministerial experiences will help Catholic youth ministers bring together their faith in the Lord Jesus, their participation in Church life, and their ministry as disciples. They will be far more than "technicians" in youth ministry practice who have the skills to run a number of events and provide a few services for no other reason than that the programs are popular with young people. Those adult leaders will be ministers of God's word and action in the community.

Competencies

The task of developing the competencies of Catholic youth ministers is made much easier when seen in light of the core competencies and specialized competencies for lay ecclesial ministers developed by a number of Catholic organizations on the national scene. In a collaborative publication, *National Certification Standards for Lay Ecclesial Ministers*, the core competencies for all Catholic lay ecclesial ministers are presented in a clear and practical format. In addition, the publication also presents the specialized competencies needed by Catholic youth ministry leaders. Dioceses, parishes, schools, youth-serving organizations, and academic institutions will find in this certification resource a solid foundation for developing comprehensive and coherent programs of formation and training for their adult youth ministry leaders. The *National Certification Standards for Lay Ecclesial Leaders* resource manual provides the Catholic youth ministry community with a set of solid criteria for establishing programs of certification in Catholic youth ministry for use in colleges, universities, and diocesan formation programs for lay ecclesial leaders. In addition, this resource offers Catholic youth ministers a framework for setting up their own learning projects to further their personal and professional competency as ministers of God's word to and with young people.

Youth ministry leaders can help their colleagues grow in faith and ministerial effectiveness by structuring youth ministry gatherings with the intention of furthering the formation and competencies of the youth ministry community. Moments of prayer at meetings could be structured to include reflection on the Scriptures, shared prayer, faith sharing, and an exploration of new prayer forms. Days of recollection could be made to include the traditional practice of *lectio divina,* faith sharing, or discussion on a theological article or book. Planning-committee meetings could include exploration of the theological principles that underlie the ministerial activities being prepared. Members could be invited to prayer while discerning God's will in making crucial decisions. Program team meetings could include some time for theological reflection on the ministerial experiences that have been shared during the day. Program evaluation meetings could include a prayerful reflection on the ministerial experience and the meaning it gives to our life and faith. When structured from the perspective of theological assumptions, the ordinary activities and experiences of the Catholic youth ministry community are effective means of faith formation and professional training for our adult youth ministry members.

Chapter Questions

1. After reflecting on the mission statement and goals of a youth ministry community, identify the basic theological principles that underlie and give form to their ministerial efforts. How do those theological assumptions find concrete expression in the training provided and the programs offered by the Catholic youth ministry community?
2. How do the theological assumptions at work in a parish's youth ministry efforts relate to the basic theological principles identified in this chapter? In what ways might that parish feel affirmed by this comparison? In what ways might the parish feel challenged to further development?
3. Identify some of the ways a Catholic youth ministry leader can be a more effective steward of the Lord's ministerial charism by explicitly attending to the basic theological principles underlying her or his endeavors in Catholic youth ministry.
4. If a parent came to you and suggested that the young people in your parish, school, or organization take part in an event sponsored by an agency outside your official Church structure (for ex-

ample, Silver Ring Thing, Youth 2000, Young Life, or youth conferences organized by a Catholic university), how would you formulate a response? What criteria would you use in making your decision?

5. Many Catholic youth ministry personnel take part in the resource days and conferences offered by nondenominational organizations such as Youth Specialties. What strategies could be employed to encourage ministry leaders to profit from those helpful experiences without bringing back programs or processes that are at variance with, or contradictory to, the theological assumptions of Catholic youth ministry and the overall goals of the local youth ministry enterprise?

Chapter 2

A Vision of Catholic Youth Ministry

Greg "Dobie" Moser

Introduction

In 1976 *A Vision of Youth Ministry* introduced a new era in ministry with Catholic young people. The document provided goals, components, and basic principles for a comprehensive approach in ministry to, with, for, and by young people. In 1997 the U.S. bishops wrote *Renewing the Vision*, affirming the direction of the previous twenty years and moving the Church's ministry forward for a changing reality.

Objectives

This chapter identifies the importance of vision as the foundation of youth ministry, reviews the framework of youth ministry provided by *Renewing the Vision*, and situates youth ministry within the context of parish life.

Companionship and Mission

Youth Ministry Rooted in Companionship

> Then Jesus called the twelve together and gave them power and authority over all demons and to cure diseases, and he sent them out to proclaim the kingdom of God and to heal. He said to them, "Take nothing for your journey, no staff, nor bag, nor bread, nor money—not even an extra tunic. . . ." They departed and went through the villages, bringing the good news and curing diseases everywhere. (Luke 9:1–6)

This guiding image of companionship, articulated in *Renewing the Vision,* is rooted in Gospel mission. It is built on the growth and development of youth ministry from its inception in the 1930s through the first *Vision of Youth Ministry* document published in 1976. That document used the story of the road to Emmaus as the guiding image for youth ministry. It offered a reminder of the power of relationships and of walking with young people to nourish and foster discipleship. The ministerial relationships rooted in the Gospel change lives and bring hope to millions of Catholic youth and adults.

Youth Ministry Rooted in Mission

Understanding that truth builds on truth and wisdom builds on wisdom, youth ministry has evolved to focus on mission. In his "Homily for World Youth Day 1995's Prayer Vigil," Pope John Paul II said it this way:

> How does Jesus send you? He promises neither sword, nor money, nor any things which the means of social communications make attractive to people today. He gives you instead grace and truth. He sends you out with the powerful message of his paschal mystery, with the truth of the cross and the resurrection. That is all he gives you, and that is all you need. (No. 17)

Through both walking with young people and helping them embrace the mission of the Gospel, Catholic youth ministry has a vision that is compelling and demanding of those who seek to be disciples of Jesus Christ.

Goals for Youth Ministry

Goal 1: "To empower young people to live as disciples of Jesus Christ in our world today" (*Renewing the Vision*, p. 9)

The first goal for youth ministry reminds us that discipleship is about how we live our faith daily in the world. It focuses on helping young people grow in their knowledge, beliefs, values, and actions to enable them to live as Christians and be witnesses to others. It is noteworthy that this is not a consumer model of Church based on coming to get the sacraments or services provided, as if choosing items from a shelf for purchase. This goal reminds us that sacraments, like our faith and Christian witness, are not objects to be received but actions to be lived.

Another important distinction for goal one is the priority of helping young people grow in their relationship with Jesus Christ. That relationship takes life within a family, within a faith community (a family of families), and within the institution of the Roman Catholic Church. The sequence does matter, as the focus is not to first socialize young people into a relationship with the institutional Church. There will be time later in their faith journey when they are able to more fully appreciate the many gifts and the structure of the universal Church.

Goal one aims to move young people from being Catholics of habit to being Catholics of experience. Knowledge, beliefs, and actions are essential ingredients for those seeking to live as authentic disciples of Jesus Christ. The goal is to know, love, and serve God through habits of the mind, habits of the heart, and habits of action. This will enable young people to know Jesus's promise, "I came that they may have life, and have it abundantly" (John 10:10).

Goal 2: "To draw young people to responsible participation in the life, mission, and work of the Catholic faith community" (*Renewing the Vision*, p. 11)

Responsible participation in the faith community is a growing and changing experience. At every age and stage of life, people bring different perspectives, gifts, limitations, and needs to the community. Determining what the responsible participation of young people looks like in every facet of community life is the work of every parish. It is fundamental that youth's role in the Church is not about having a segregated youth group with its own Mass and separate programs, a false attraction to some youth and adults alike who may not be comfortable around each other. The challenge instead is to integrate youth into the life and mission of the parish, always with the goal of inviting them into the joys and struggles of faithful discipleship. "The ministry of community life is not only *what* we do (activity), but *who* we are (identity) and *how* we interact (relationships)" (*Renewing the Vision*, p. 34).

The ministry and mission of the Church are shared by all through Baptism. This rich understanding of community includes people of every age, background, and experience. As baptized Christians, all are welcome and needed to help us live as a community. When people of any age or group are absent from the community, we are incomplete. This Christian community exists turning outward, for the good of the world, as a sign of the power and life that we share through Jesus Christ and celebrate with one another.

Goal 3: "To foster the total personal and spiritual growth of each young person" (*Renewing the Vision*, p. 15)

Goal three reminds us to start where the young people are, versus where we would like them to be, on their journey of faith. Like Catholics of all ages, teens vary widely in their knowledge, experience, and practice of faith. Often they have experiences of the sacred and holy but have not thought about them in such terms or reflected on larger possible meanings. Bob McCarty, the general editor of this publication, uses the phrase "experience rich and language poor" to frame the perspective that many youth bring to religion. Teens have a hunger for God and are quite ready to ask difficult questions. Goal three directs us to help teens make the connection for naming and living life's questions in a Church that is big enough to welcome them with their doubts, truths, gifts, struggles, and insights.

Goal three fosters the development of a Catholic worldview that respects the dignity of human life, recalling that every person is made in God's image and likeness. That worldview is based on the Gospel values of love, peace, mercy, and justice as the heart of what it means to be a disciple of Jesus. A Catholic worldview equips adolescents with a basic frame of reference from which to work through the day-to-day experiences of love, forgiveness, and intimacy, while providing a foundation for growth and understanding as the complex realities of life (for example, war, poverty, violence, suffering, science, and technology) unfold. The challenge of offering youth a Catholic worldview is not to answer life's complex questions for them or to coerce them to do as we say, but to listen to them and engage them as we reflect the truths of our Tradition and teachings as a Church committed to furthering the Reign of God.

Youth Ministry and Parish Life

Imagine that a person with no religious background or affiliation wandered into your parish hall on a Sunday morning during doughnut-and-coffee time. Curious to know what was going on, he asked a number of those present the following questions: "What does it mean to be a member of your parish? What is it that you do that is important and gives you your identity as a member of your parish?"

It is quite likely that people would give the following answers:
- We pray and worship together, celebrating the Eucharist and the sacraments.
- We do acts of service and justice in our parish, our community, and beyond.
- We gather as a community to celebrate, serve, support, and nourish one another.
- We reach out to those who are suffering and offer pastoral care to those who are hurting.
- We have leadership in many forms and organizations throughout the parish.
- We educate people of all ages on the meaning of who we are and what we believe.
- We evangelize by telling and retelling the Gospel story of hope and life.
- We advocate for Catholic values in public life and serve as a voice for the voiceless.
- We have fun and enjoy gathering around the table and supporting family life.
- We uphold the dignity of human life in all its forms, conditions, and ages.

Intrigued, the guest then asks, "How does one becomes a member of your parish community, and how long does the membership last?" The coordinator of youth ministry (CYM) responds that "one joins when baptized and is a member for life, until death, which we believe is eternal life."

Amazed, the guest asks, "Who is responsible to do all those things, and how do you take such a comprehensive approach with people of different ages?" The CYM informs the guest that the ministry just described is the ministry of the baptized, done by all members of the community according to their time, talents, and treasures. As for the comprehensive approach, each area is done according to the developmental life stage of the people involved. Education and formation take on different looks for the preschooler, the fourth grader, the teenager, and the adult, according to the desired goals and the best strategies or methods to achieve those goals. Pastoral care is different when dealing with a family that is suffering the loss of a member or with a member who is working through the pain of separation or divorce. Prayer involves sacraments celebrated in the parish community, prayers of support offered between parishioners during difficult times, or prayer services at the parish youth ministry retreat.

The responses to the guest's questions articulate the *Renewing the Vision* components—things that parishioners know instinctively as the heart of parish life. The components—advocacy, catechesis, community life, evangelization, justice and service, leadership development, pastoral care, and prayer and worship—covered in later chapters in greater depth, are the essence of parish life. This comprehensive framework is more about parish life than it is about youth ministry. How each of the components is animated by the community for all the age-groups present in the community reframes youth ministry as an integral part of parish life. In that way the question becomes, How does your parish do comprehensive ministry with all the different age-groups in your parish? Put another way, How does your parish love and care for its young people and their families while helping them grow as disciples of Jesus Christ?

The comprehensive approach to parish life does not readily accept that at a certain age or stage in life, in this case adolescence, the Church quits caring for its young people and blindly hopes that if we lose them, they will magically return when they marry or when they have a child who needs to be baptized.

It is noteworthy to mention that every parish has its own collective identity, or charism. Therefore, it is quite common that the strengths of the parish are also strengths in youth ministry and that the weaknesses in parish life are present in youth ministry as well. Parishes that have a strong identity with social justice often do a great job of integrating teenagers into their social-justice efforts, thus their youth ministry efforts may be particularly strong in that component. Conversely, parishes that do not value adult education and lifelong learning often struggle with adolescent catechesis or parent-youth education events because they are not a common part or practice of their parish experience.

Comprehensive Themes

Pope John Paul II, in *I Came That They Might Have Life* (1994), describes well the task and vision of youth ministry:

> Your task will be to help your parishes, dioceses, associations, and movements to be truly open to the personal, social, and spiritual needs of young people. You will have to find ways of involving young people in projects and activities of formation, spirituality, and service, giving them responsibility for themselves and their work, and taking care to avoid isolating them and their apostolate from the rest of the ecclesial community. Young people need to be able to see the practical relevance of their efforts to meet the real needs of people, especially the poor and neglected. They should also be able to see that their apostolate belongs fully to the Church's mission in the world. (P. 201)

The comprehensive themes of *Renewing the Vision* are also the themes of parish life. Consider how those themes apply to youth ministry in your setting, as well as how they apply to all aspects of parish life.

Developmentally Appropriate

Effective ministry with teenagers recognizes the specific tasks and challenges of adolescence and makes a determined effort to respond through a wide range of youth ministry efforts.

Family Friendly

"The home is the primary context for sharing, celebrating, and living the Catholic faith, and we are partners with parents in developing the faith life of their adolescent children. . . . The Church's ministry . . . should lead young people into a deeper faith life within their own families. In other words, ministry with adolescents should not take adolescents away from the family, but rather foster family life" (*Renewing the Vision*, p. 21).

Intergenerational

Connecting young people with people of all ages provides an opportunity for adolescents to give and receive while gaining from the experience of others. By working with those who are different from themselves, teens discover their roles more clearly and grow to recognize markers along the way that will guide them in their journey of faith.

Multicultural

"Ministry with adolescents recognizes, values, and responds to the diverse ethnic and cultural backgrounds and experiences that exist among adolescents and develops culturally responsive and inclusive programming to address these needs" (*Renewing the Vision*, pp. 22–23). This value embraces the concept of unity in diversity, valuing what every culture brings to enrich and animate the universal Church.

Communitywide Collaboration

"Community collaboration means building partnerships among families, schools, churches, and organizations that mobilize the community in a common effort to build a healthier community life and to promote positive adolescent development" (*Renewing the Vision*, p. 24). The Church is not alone in its caring for young people, and it needs to work strategically with others on behalf of youth and families.

Leadership

Effective youth ministry animates the gifts and resources of the community to work together to achieve the three goals of youth ministry. "Ministry coordinators alert the whole community to its responsibility for young people, draw forth the community's gifts and resources, and encourage and empower the community to minister with young people" (*Renewing the Vision*, pp. 24–25).

Flexible and Adaptable Programming

A comprehensive approach to youth ministry incorporates "a variety of approaches to reach all adolescents and their families, including parish, school, and community-wide programs" (*Renewing the Vision*, p. 25). There is no single program, approach, or youth movement that can fully achieve the goals of youth ministry. Therefore many different programs, experiences, and strategies enable parishes to adjust to local needs in order to do what is most effective with youth and families.

The Components of Youth Ministry

In addition to the seven themes noted previously, *Renewing the Vision* identifies eight components as essential for comprehensive ministry with youth. Though the following chapters will focus more specifically on those components, a brief description is appropriate here:
- *Advocacy* challenges the faith and social community to consider how well the needs of young people are being met and how well young people are integrated into the community.

- *Catechesis* fosters youth's relationship with Jesus while deepening their understanding, practice, and knowledge of the Catholic faith.
- *Community life* nurtures the faith of young people by creating meaningful relationships with their peers and with caring adults, and by fully integrating young people into the community.
- *Evangelization* proclaims and witnesses to the Reign of God made flesh in Jesus and invites young people to enter into relationship with Jesus and live as his disciples.
- *Justice and service* encourages young people to live fully Jesus's command to love one another, responding to the human needs of the local and global community while working to transform the social structures that perpetuate injustice.
- *Leadership development* affirms the gifts of adults and youth for ministry and creates opportunities for those gifts to be realized and utilized.
- *Pastoral care* promotes healthy adolescent development, supports the family, and responds to young people in need.
- *Prayer and worship* celebrates the faith of young people through personal and communal prayer and liturgical experiences, and incorporates young people in the sacramental and worship life of the faith community.

Comprehensive youth ministry requires an awareness of the content of our faith, the practices of our faith, and the actions required to live as disciples in the world. It requires a vision of youth ministry that is compelling and demanding, one with high expectations, backed up with a plan for how to get there. That vision is inclusive of our rich Catholic heritage, which includes our history and theology, liturgy and sacraments, experience of the Church, understanding of the sacred Scriptures, morality, social teaching, spirituality, ecumenism, and more. Comprehensive youth ministry not only animates and evangelizes young people, it also serves as a foundation to help young people grow on their lifelong journey into the mystery of our Catholic faith, gradually discovering why we believe what we do and practice as we do. This vision gives young people a deep and genuine hope and the resilience of character to imagine a future of discipleship lived in the world.

Chapter Questions

1. How would each of the following groups in your parish setting describe the vision of youth ministry?
   • the pastor and staff
   • parents and teens
   • the youth ministry coordinator and adult youth ministry leaders
   • other key people
2. How does your parish vision of youth ministry connect with the Church's comprehensive approach in *Renewing the Vision?* Where are the natural connecting points as well as the possible conflicts?
3. What resources (budget, personnel, materials) does your parish designate to youth ministry and how does that relate to the priority of youth ministry in your parish?
4. Evaluate the leadership structure for youth ministry in your parish. How is the vision of youth ministry shared with all the leaders?
5. What do you see as possible roles for adult and youth leadership in youth ministry in your setting?

Chapter 3

The State of Catholic Adolescents

Sean Reynolds

Introduction

Adults who hope to effectively speak to the hearts of young people need to become amateur cultural anthropologists, with eyes and ears attuned to information about the lives and cultures of young people, constantly learning, critiquing assumptions, and formulating hypotheses about their thinking and living. This work is ongoing, never completed, and part of what makes youth ministry so fascinating.

Objectives

This chapter looks broadly at young people in the United States, surfacing significant societal trends; focusing on recent research regarding youth and religion, then on the Catholic experience; and suggesting implications and applications for youth ministers.

Young Catholics in the United States

Young Catholics are largely inseparable from the general fabric of American life and culture. In most respects they mirror the general youth population. As such they are part of what has become widely identified as the Millennial Generation, they are products of postmodern culture, and they reflect the health and well-being (or lack thereof) of U.S. adolescents.

Five distinct generational cohorts inhabit the United States today, and the Millennials are the most recent. Their precise beginning and endpoints, and in some cases their official titles, may be debated, but the reality of fundamentally different characteristics of each is not. Each generation has its unique identity, which blurs during the transition years into the subsequent generation:

Generation	**Born** (approx.)
G.I. Generation, Seniors	1901–1924
Silent Generation, Builders	1925–1942
Baby Boomers	1943–1960
Generation X, Baby Busters	1961–1981
Millennials, Generation Y, Mosaics	1982–200?

(Neil Howe and William Strauss,
Millennials Rising, p. 15; George Barna, *Real Teens*, p. 12)

Characteristics of the Millennial Generation

George Barna, a Christian researcher, provides the following snapshot of Millennial youth in his book *Real Teens:*

- Their lifestyles are an eclectic combination of traditional and alternative activities.
- They are the first generation among whom a majority will exhibit a nonlinear style of thinking—a mosaic, connect-the-dots however-you-choose approach.
- Their relationships are much more racially integrated and fluid than any we have seen in U.S. history.
- Their core values are the result of a cut-and-paste mosaic of feelings, facts, principles, experiences and lessons.
- Their primary information and connection—the Internet—is the most bizarre, inclusive and ever-changing pastiche of information ever relied upon by humankind.
- The central spiritual tenets that provide substance to their faith are a customized blend of multiple-faith views and religious practices.

(P. 17)

Barna goes on to make some comparisons between Millennials and their immediate Gen X predecessors, stating that Millennials tend to

- be more upbeat—they are less cynical, less skeptical and less pessimistic
- be more interested in developing a meaningful career and doing what must be achieved to facilitate a viable career
- view education as an irreplaceable preparation for life, rather than a means of proving their worthiness and gaining acceptance from their parents

- consider religion, spirituality and faith to be a positive dimension of life, but neither central nor critical for fulfillment
- exhibit less emotional sensitivity—they take a joke, handle criticism and understand the context of abandonment more readily
- feel more vitally connected to other people and to their culture

(P. 23)

In their book *Millennials Rising,* authors Neil Howe and William Strauss suggest that America can expect to see more evidence that Millennials are

- *Special.* Older generations have inculcated in Millennials the sense that they are, collectively, vital to the nation and to their parents' sense of purpose.
- *Sheltered.* Millennials are the focus of the most sweeping youth safety movement in American history.
- *Confident.* Millennial teens are beginning to equate good news for themselves with good news for their country. They often boast about their generation's power and potential.
- *Team-oriented.* Millennials are developing strong team instincts and tight peer bonds.
- *Achieving.* Millennials are on track to become the best-educated and best-behaved adults in the nation's history.
- *Pressured.* Pushed to study hard, avoid personal risks, and take full advantage of the collective opportunities adults are offering them, Millennials feel a "trophy kid" pressure to excel.
- *Conventional.* Taking pride in their improving behavior and more comfortable with their parents values than any other generation in living memory, Millennials support convention—the idea that social rules can help.

(Pp. 43–44)

Taken as a composite, those characteristics present a profoundly hopeful profile of Millennials. If Howe and Strauss are correct, and the Millennials indeed are slated to become the next great generation, youth ministers may play a vital role in shaping their values, perspectives, and faith—and in so doing, helping to shape a better future.

Implications for Ministry

Ministry is a response to human hungers for God, faith, community, and service, and on the whole, the Millennials are not a very hungry generation, unless it's a hunger for a break in the action. They are, in fact, sated with options and opportunities of all kinds: entertainment, athletics, electronic communications, civic and community involvements, an array of educational and travel opportunities, and more. This has been aptly described as "option overload," and results in overstimulated, overscheduled, pressurized people whose root hunger is not for another program or project but simply for Sabbath rest.

Youth ministry leaders need to meet those young people in their genuine hungers—resisting the impulse to add to the melee of multiple pushes, pulls, and pressures—and provide them with oases of rest and spiritual rejuvenation.

Ministry with Postmoderns

One can only understand postmodern culture in contrast to the "modern" period that preceded it. Modern thinking has its roots in the historical period of the Enlightenment, and came into its full flower in the scientific and industrial revolutions. Modernism assumes that human intellect will prevail when applied to virtually any problem or situation. It exalts humankind and holds fast to faith in human ability to make a better world.

Postmodernism is a reaction to that way of thinking and living, and emerged out of the failure of modernism to deliver on its promise. The scientific and industrial revolutions, though replete with amazing inventions and fantastic scientific breakthroughs, also brought nuclear weapons, environmental degradation, and ever more efficient ways for people to do violence to one another. In the postmodern world, objectivity is out, subjectivity is in; absolutes are out, and everything is relative; absolute, objective truth is out, and subjective relativism is in.

The Millennials are the first generation to have been reared in a postmodern culture. This suggests that Millennial youth will generally have a predisposition toward a postmodern mindset, which might be characterized by their being

- more experiential than rational
- more spiritual than scientific
- more tolerant and accepting of diversity and pluralism
- more altruistic than egocentric
- more community-minded and group-oriented, and less individualistic

Moreover, they will likely

- believe that truth is relative, and that there are few or no absolutes
- value creativity over functionality
- be comfortable thinking globally, not just locally
- appreciate and demand authenticity over relevance
- question everything and approach life with a deep skepticism

(Adapted from Tony Jones, *Postmodern Youth Ministry,* pp. 30–37)

Implications for Youth Ministry

Youth ministry leaders who work with postmodern youth face the following challenges.

The Primacy of Personal Experience

Logical, rational, discursive arguments designed to convince are generally ineffective. Significant development, learning, and growth result from direct, personal, and meaningful experiences.

Authenticity over Relevance

Postmoderns are hungry for authenticity, for personal and meaningful connections with sources of deep and substantial wisdom. As such, they are typically more open to traditional forms of piety and worship, provided those forms are participative and experiential, not theoretical or didactic.

Stories v. The Story

Postmoderns generally are suspicious of any religion, ideology, or story that claims to be the one source of absolute truth and salvation for all people. Conversely, they respond well to specific stories that reveal truth with a small "t" in specific circumstances, such as in witness talks or faith-sharing settings.

Openness to Personal, Spiritual, Mystical Experience

Postmoderns are singularly open to spiritual experiences and are much more responsive to opportunities to express their spirituality than were their predecessors. This can take the form of interest in the sacraments, devotions, sacramentals, new ways to pray (provided they're not "gimmicky" or transparently trying hard to be relevant), and authentic, heartfelt communal worship.

Hunger for Clarity and Ultimates

Awash in a culture where everything is relative and there are apparently no ultimate truths, postmoderns are attracted to those sources of authentic truth that seem most solid and trustworthy. Traditional religions like Catholicism, with a long history and rich, deep traditions, can offer that kind of solidity. As a reaction to the uncertainty of their culture, postmoderns may turn to traditional religions for clear, definitive, black-and-white answers to life's questions. Taken to the extreme, that tendency can result in an unhealthy rigidity and a rejection of any ambiguity, or "gray," in religion, life, and faith.

Boomers Ministering with Millennials

The Baby Boom generation is generally modernist in mindset, whereas Millennials are nearly unanimously postmodern. This poses unique challenges to Boomers' ministering with Millennials: their assumptions about life, communication, reality, and religion may be quite alien to postmodern youth. Boomer youth ministers cannot assume that the approaches and methods that worked for them will work for postmoderns; rather, they need to become humble students of postmodern culture and critically examine their ministry practices, with input and feedback from postmoderns on their effectiveness.

These profiles of Millennial, postmodern youth are at best snapshots of general characteristics. There is much to be hopeful about and grateful for, yet it would be a mistake to assume that all is well, or that all young people in this generation enjoy the sunny existence that Howe and Strauss describe. In fact, the bright light of those glowing reports and predictions may well cause us to lose sight of at-risk youth who struggle simply to exist in the shadows and at the margins of our society, including groups such as these:

- immigrant youth, especially those with little or no command of the language
- young people living in poverty, especially those in urban and rural areas
- youth and families enmeshed in substance abuse
- youth with disabilities
- youth who suffer from depression, and who struggle mightily with the pressure they feel to achieve and succeed

Moreover, we have yet to understand how profoundly the post–9-11 world will affect the Millennials. Until September 11, 2001, Millennials thrived in an American society that seemed safe and utterly prosperous. They grew up during what has been described as one of the greatest economic booms in history, in the most affluent and powerful nation on earth. Now they experience nearly daily news of threats of terrorism and a troubled economy with daunting prospects. It is impossible to predict how this will affect the Millennials—their dreams, their hopes, their plans, and how they perceive the world. Youth ministry leaders need to pay close attention to young people and to societal trends in this regard so as to respond with appropriate pastoral care.

Further Implications for Ministry

Just as the U.S. bishops, in *Renewing the Vision,* call for a comprehensive framework of youth ministry that partners with others within and outside the Church on behalf of young people, so too are youth ministry leaders called out of a parochial vision of youth ministry and into a larger world of concern. This includes partnering with parents, civic organizations, other churches, health-care agencies, and the like in order to respond to the challenges of early sexual maturation, STDs, substance abuse, teenage pregnancy, teen obesity, and poverty. Obviously, in the face of such societal problems, isolated actions by individuals will be much less effective than orchestrated, communitywide efforts. Youth ministry leaders would do well to assess their patterns of cooperation and collaboration with other youth-serving individuals and organizations. If one's pattern of activity includes little or no collaborative effort, it's likely that change is warranted.

Religion and American Youth

Equipped with the preceding broad perspectives on youth in the United States, we can now turn our sights a bit more narrowly on U.S. youth and religion. The most current relevant research is available through the *National Study on Youth and Religion*. At the time of this writing, some results of this landmark research have been made available, and more is anxiously anticipated. Following is a summary of some of the findings to date.

Constructive v. At-Risk Behaviors

The study found a significant positive correlation between religious involvement and healthy and constructive involvements such as volunteerism, student government, exercise, and personal fitness. Young people who are significantly involved in their faith were also found to be less likely to be involved in a variety of at-risk behaviors, such as substance abuse, dangerous driving practices, crime, violence, and problems at school (adapted from "Religion and American Adolescent Delinquency, Risk Behaviors, and Constructive Social Activities," report no. 1, pp. 7–8).

Positive v. Negative Attitudes About Life

The research clearly indicates that religious youth are apt to have significantly higher self-esteem and more positive attitudes about life in general than their less religious peers. Regular attendance (at church services), high importance of faith, and years spent in religious youth groups are clearly associated with high self-esteem and positive self-attitudes. The report goes on to comment specifically about Catholics: "Catholic twelfth graders differed most from the nonreligious, being significantly more likely to have positive attitudes toward themselves, feel proud of something, feel hopeful, feel like their lives are useful, feel good to be alive, enjoy school, and be conventional in their behavior" (adapted from "Religion and the Life Attitudes and Self-Images of American Adolescents," report no. 2, p. 8).

Effects of Family Religious Involvement

The research indicates a significant positive correlation between family religious involvement (including frequency of family religious activity, parental religious service attendance, and parental prayer) and markers indicating stronger family relationships than those in families that are not religiously involved. For instance, a significant connection is found between weekly parental worship attendance and the following indicators of healthy family relations:

- regular evening meals together
- mothers who know most things about the parents of their children's close friends and who know who their children are with when they are not at home
- fathers whom they aspire to be like and of whom they think highly
- fathers who are supportive and don't abruptly cancel plans with them

Similarly, prayer makes a difference: youth report having stronger relationships with mothers and fathers who pray more than once a day (adapted from "Family Religious Involvement and the Quality of Family Relationships for Early Adolescents," report no. 4, pp. 5 and 6). Moreover, the research suggests that mothers and fathers in religiously involved families of early adolescents have stronger relationships with each other than those in families that are not religiously involved. The report goes on to state that "family religious activity, parental attendance (at weekly worship), and parental prayer are often significantly associated with positive parental relationships" ("Family Religious Involvement and the Quality of Parental Relationships for Families with Early Adolescents," report no. 5, p. 6).

Alienation from Organized Religion

The research calls into question one of the most persistent stereotypes about U.S. teenagers: that they are alienated from organized religion, and that this alienation is on the rise. The great majority of U.S. twelfth graders—about two-thirds of them—do not evidence alienation from or hostility toward organized religion. Somewhat surprisingly, only 15 percent report such alienation or hostility, and another 15 percent appear simply to be disengaged or disinterested (adapted from "Are American Youth Alienated from Organized Religion?" report no. 6, p. 5).

Implications for Ministry

Clearly this research stands as a powerful testament to the profoundly positive influence religion has on the lives of those young people who are involved in it. The research also strongly suggests that the more involved in their faith young people and their families are, the greater the positive effects are that they enjoy in their individual and family lives. For Millennial youth and their families, who already are predisposed toward seeking positive ways to enhance the quality of their lives, this research can pose a compelling argument for the efficacy of religious involvement. Indeed, religious involvement and practices appear to be significant bellwethers of family and adolescent health and well-being. Finally, the research strongly points up the inextricable link between adolescent faith and the faith of parents and family. To minister with youth independent of a family perspective, ignoring the powerful influence of parents on their children, would be foolhardy. This reinforces the wisdom of the national movement in the Catholic Church, already well under way, toward prioritizing adult faith formation and intergenerational approaches to faith formation and ministry.

U.S. Catholic Youth: An Emerging Profile

It is possible to craft a profile of Catholic young people based on what we know about Millennial, postmodern youth, their health and well-being, and their religiosity. The following descriptions are not prescriptive, nor do they apply to all Catholic adolescents. Rather, they may serve as a general profile of Catholic young people in the United States.

Believers, But Not Necessarily Disciples

This generation of American Catholics is awash in a sea of choices: hero figures, philosophies, values, and religions. If there is one unifying secular backdrop for all these, it is the potent mix of consumerism, materialism, and individualism that are the hallmarks of modern American society. The gentle invitation to follow Jesus can easily be overwhelmed by a cacophony of competing invitations in the form of powerful images and messages, all selling something. It is in this context that youth ministers must find ways to be heard, above the din, to invite young people to follow Jesus.

Tolerant of Other Beliefs

Postmodern Catholic youth have grown up in a pluralistic culture offering a wide array of religions, philosophies, values, and opportunities. Their typical default position on such would be that it's up to the individual to decide "what works for me." They are therefore typically quite tolerant of different denominations, faiths, beliefs, and value systems. Conversely, the notion that any one of those might claim to have a corner on truth may well be off-putting to postmodern Catholic youth—such a claim could well be perceived as arrogant and uninformed.

Eclectic in Religious Practices

For postmodern Catholic youth, the general criterion used to assess the value of a religious practice would be its personal, individual significance and meaning. Generally, Catholic youth will be open to virtually any religious practice, provided it is personal, meaningful, and experiential.

Authentic Religious Experience

Relevance is out; authenticity is in. Transparently superficial glitz and gimmicks are written off as cheap, thin, or lacking depth or substance. Conversely, experiences that express substance, depth, longstanding tradition, and truth with a capital "T" are attractive. Young people who have been steeped in a relativistic culture are interested in what seems solid and lasting.

Open to Spirituality and Mystical Experiences

The postmodern penchant for validating truth through one's own personal experience can represent a powerful entry point for youth ministry leaders if they can provide opportunities for personal and meaningful experiences of prayer and worship. Millennial Catholic youth are uniquely open to the sacred, and hunger for transcendence, for the sacred, for something more deep and real and authentic than what might be found on television or on the Web.

Conformists Who Appreciate Authority

Generally, Millennial Catholic youth default to a posture of acceptance of legitimate authority. This generation looks for, and looks up to, leaders who are genuine and authentic, and whose authority is legitimate and authorized. They are good followers and team players, having been part of many kinds of teams throughout their childhood.

Their Parents' Children

Millennial Catholic youth generally feel tremendous support from their parents, trust them, look up to them, listen to them, and follow their lead. Obviously, that is a tremendous advantage if one's parents are believing Catholics who daily and intentionally live their faith. This points to the critical value of adult faith formation: as parents' faith goes, so goes the faith of their children.

Capable of Holding Apparently Irreconcilable Positions

Whether due to brain development still under construction or to their relativized notions of truth, Catholic young people can hold positions that to their elders may seem mutually irreconcilable. For instance, a Catholic youth may express utter devotion to Pope John Paul II, and in the same breath, be absolutely in favor of women's ordination.

Disinterested in Conservative v. Liberal Ideological Conflicts

For Millennial Catholic youth, Vatican Council II feels like ancient history. The ideological arguments resulting from the reforms of Vatican II that absorb the attention of many Boomer Catholics are for Millennial Catholic youth akin to debating women's suffrage. They have grown up in churches where the liturgy has always been in English, women have always had significant leadership roles, and there aren't many priests or religious. They don't "get" the angst and umbrage that their elders sometimes express; they're much more interested in making something personal, meaningful, and significant happen in people's lives.

Volunteer Service Providers

Today's Catholic youth have grown up in an era when voluntarism and service became the norm rather than the exception. The methodology of service learning has impacted classrooms and ministry settings alike. Service used to be an altruistic option; now it's the norm for teens. As such, service can provide the context for a powerful encounter with God, as often is the case on mission trips, at work camps, and the like.

Busy, Busy, Busy

Many Catholic young people are victims of "option overload": a by-product of living in an affluent society with an overabundance of athletic, educational, entertainment, social, and religious opportunities, many of which are positive, healthy, and enjoyable. Catholic youth, like their parents, hunger for a break in the action, a bit of solitude, and time for reflection.

Plugged into Electronic Media

Millennial Catholic youth have, from their youngest years, been surrounded, in fact, inundated, with electronic media. They are connected with one another electronically through computers and cell phones, by instant messaging, e-mailing, and text messaging.

Further, they have been raised on nonstop, fast-paced images ("videocized"), with video and music options only clicks away on computers, MP3 players, and the like. They are generally savvy and sophisticated users of technology; friends, entertainment, information, and merchandise are mere seconds and only a mouse click or two away. Minimally, youth ministry leaders must stay abreast of technology simply to avoid being left behind in normal conversation. Ideally, however, they will dedicate themselves to becoming adept at the use of technology so as to communicate effectively with young people on their terms.

Conclusion

As we look to the future, we can do so with some measure of hope and optimism, based on all that we know about Millennial youth. On the whole they are a hopeful and optimistic generation. They are well-educated, achievement-oriented, can-do people. They are open to faith and religious experience, are tolerant of differences, and take volunteer service for granted. They are team players, sophisticated users of technology, and well connected to their families. They may in fact be "the next great generation."

However, they are also stressed from overly busy lives. They are maturing physically long before they mature psychologically, socially, or emotionally. The safe, peaceful, and prosperous world they were born into now feels threatening and unsafe. Their electronic world daily serves up a vast smorgasbord of values and options, some healthy and wholesome, many neutral, and some downright destructive. Some of them are seriously at risk for significant health problems. Some are ensnared in poverty, are immigrants new to the country and language, are pregnant, or are afflicted by STDs.

It is in this rich and complex mix of hope and challenge that we hear again Pope John Paul II's prayer:

> This is what is needed: *a Church for young people,* which will know how to speak to their heart and enkindle, comfort, and inspire enthusiasm in it with the joy of the gospel. (*Messages of His Holiness Pope John Paul II for the XXXII World Day of Prayer for Vocations,* no. 2)

Chapter Questions

1. What information from this chapter do you find new, surprising, or challenging?
2. What information from this chapter seems most urgent or relevant to a parish's ministry with young people?
3. What other questions come to mind as you think about the information in this chapter? What other areas would you like to explore?
4. Based on the information in this chapter, how could a parish approach ministry with young people differently?

Chapter 4

Young Disciples: Adolescent Christian Discipleship and Faith Practices

Jeffrey Kaster

Introduction

Christian apprenticeship begins with a response to Christ's call to "follow me" (Matthew 4:19). The call to Christian discipleship is fundamentally a call to conversion. The *General Directory for Catechesis* suggests that Jesus, the master, formed the disciples through an apprenticeship in Christian life (cf. no. 137). The Church needs now more than ever to start an apprenticing process "to empower [youth and adults] to live as disciples of Jesus Christ in the world today" (*Renewing the Vision*, p. 9).

Objectives

This chapter discusses the meaning of Christian discipleship through the lens of Church documents and the Scriptures and then explores a process of apprenticing adolescent Christian disciples.

Church Documents on Discipleship

For thirty years universal and national Church documents have highlighted the process of making disciples within the context of the Church's mission of evangelization. Some examples from recent Church documents help locate the formation of adolescent Christian disciples within the heart of the Church's mission of evangelization.

Pope Paul VI's apostolic letter *On Evangelization in the Modern World (Evangelii Nuntiandi)* (1975) focused the Church's mission on evangelization. Although that document does not specifically discuss discipleship, it makes two points about evangelization that directly relate to the process of forming disciples. The first point is that evangelization includes a radical conversion (no. 10). This encompasses a transformation of both individuals and cultures (nos. 19–20). The second point is that those who are evangelized go on to be evangelizers (no. 24). They make up a community of disciples who participate in the mission of evangelizing (no. 13). *Go and Make Disciples: A National Plan and Strategy for Catholic Evangelization in the United States* specifically names the formation of Christian disciples as a goal for the Church in the United States.

The *Catechism of the Catholic Church* relates the process of making disciples to catechesis: "Quite early on, the name *catechesis* was given to the totality of the Church's efforts to make disciples, to help [people] believe that Jesus is the Son of God so that believing they might have life in his name, and to educate and instruct them in this life, thus building up the body of Christ[2]" (no. 4).

The *General Directory for Catechesis* explains this catechetical moment of making disciples as "an apprenticeship in the whole Christian life[3]" (no. 63).

Renewing the Vision adds a new first goal to Catholic youth ministry in the United States: "To empower young people to live as disciples of Jesus Christ in our world today" (p. 9).

Those documents highlight the Church's renewed focus on forming adult and adolescent Christian disciples through a catechumenal model. Christian discipleship includes a conversion, an apprenticeship in Christian living, and becoming a community on mission. It is interesting to note that although those documents clearly call for a renewed effort in forming disciples, nowhere in the documents is the term *discipleship* extensively defined. Perhaps that is one reason why adults working in youth ministry are confused about its meaning and manifestation.

Scriptural Views of Discipleship

The New Testament provides important insights about the meaning of discipleship. The Greek word for "to follow" (*akoloutheo*) occurs ninety-one times in the New Testament, while the word for "disciple" (*mathetes*) occurs 261 times (Timothy O'Connell, *Making Disciples,* p. 13). Some, like Peter, Mary Magdalene, and Anna, respond to that call and follow Jesus, while others, like the rich young man in the Gospel of Luke, turn away. A foundational understanding of discipleship is that it is a response to Christ's call. It begins with Christ's initiative (his teaching, preaching, healing, and call), but requires freedom to accept or reject the invitation. Jesus does not force Peter, Mary, Anna, or the rich young man to follow him. Following Christ means learning from the master. *Mathetes* literally means "an apprentice or learner." Thus, a Christian disciple is a person who freely responds to Christ's call and enters into an apprenticeship learning relationship with Christ that shapes that person's entire life.

Aaron Milavec explains the importance of this notion of apprenticeship. He observes that in all four Gospels, "Jesus was received as a master apprenticing disciples. The Greek designation for Jesus was *didaskalos* (master), and his principle activity was *didaskein* (to apprentice)." Milavec suggests that the New Testament English translations of *didaskalos* as "teacher" and *didaskein* as "to teach" miss the profound impact that such a master would have on the life orientation of the disciple. Milavec argues that Jesus's primary activity was apprenticing disciples (*To Empower as Jesus Did*, pp. 83–84).

What Is an Apprentice?

A marvelous children's story, A *Single Shard,* by Linda Sue Park, can provide important information about how we might think about apprenticing adolescent Christian disciples. The setting for the story is twelfth-century Korea, where a master potter named Min meets an orphaned homeless boy named Tree-ear, who seeks to become the potter's apprentice. What follows is a basic outline of Tree-ear's apprenticeship:

> Tree-ear is captivated by the art of pottery and seeks to become an apprentice. Tree-ear watched the potter Min day after day. Tree-ear marveled at the work of Min and dreams of throwing a clay pot on the wheel. After Tree-ear accidentally breaks a pot, Min agrees to accept nine days of work from him.
>
> The first task Min gives Tree-ear is to cut wood. The first day of chopping wood brought bloody blisters on his hands, scrapes, and exhaustion. The second day was much the same. After nine days Min accepts Tree-ear as his apprentice.

The second task Min gives Tree-ear is digging clay. At first Tree-ear got his spade stuck in the clay, but gradually he learned the skill of digging clay.

The third task Min gives Tree-ear is draining clay. That included stirring, sieving, settling, and bailing the clay. This was repeated any number of times until Min rubbed the purified clay between his fingers and was satisfied with its quality. Sometimes Tree-ear would drain and sieve the clay seven or eight times. It took Tree-ear many months to acquire the touch of his master.

Like many good stories, it happens that Tree-ear goes on an arduous journey. He travels many days to the capital city to help Min receive a royal commission from the emperor for his finest work. On this journey bandits attack Tree-ear and destroy two fine pots Min was sending to the emperor. Tree-ear recovers one single shard of pottery that shows Min's excellent work. To Tree-ear's surprise, the emperor gives Min a royal commission based on the quality of work shown in the single shard. Linda Sue Park ends the story with Tree-ear becoming a master potter himself.

This story beautifully illustrates three steps in the apprenticeship process. First, the apprentice must want to learn the craft. It must be the apprentice's heart's desire. Second, the apprentice practices the trade. This practice is hard work. Eventually, through practice, the apprentice develops the touch of the master. Third, the successful apprentice goes on to be a master in his own right. The master knows that it takes years of practice in an apprenticeship before one can become a master. The role of the master is not only to pass on the practices of the tradition, but also to add something new. Min, the master potter, was thoroughly committed to creating the best art possible. Both Min and Tree-ear mastered the tradition, and both Min and Tree-ear brought something new to the tradition. Those same three steps can be applied to the apprenticing of Christian disciples.

Apprenticing Adolescent Christian Disciples

Step One: Response to Christ's Call

The first and most important characteristic of a Christian disciple is the first step. Christian apprenticeship begins with a response to Christ's call to "follow me" (Matthew 4:18). The *General Directory for Catechesis* identifies this as part of the conversion process: a "fundamental option" that "is the basis for the whole Christian life of the Lord's disciple[4]" (no. 56b). The essential characteristic of a Christian apprentice is a choice to follow in the footsteps of Christ. The apprentice is captivated by Christ and Christian living and wants to learn more. The first step is an attraction to Christ and the Christian message. Without that first step, apprenticeship in Christian discipleship cannot begin.

The first step demands personal freedom. It cannot be coerced; it must be a free response. Cardinal Avery Dulles provides wonderful insight into the notion of the freedom needed for Christian discipleship:

> Our notion of the freedom of the Christian must be formed in the light of Christ's own sovereign freedom. Essentially, I would maintain, freedom is the power to act out of a deliberated choice, in view of the perceived goodness of that which is chosen. The Christian's freedom, like that of Jesus, will consist characteristically of choices that correspond to the known will of God. Subjection to the will of another, even God's will, could be servile if motivated by fear of punishment or hope of reward. Submission achieves full freedom to the extent that it proceeds from love. Love, in the theological sense of the term, is a spiritual act that cannot be compelled. Nothing, then, that proceeds from love can be anything but free. (*A Church to Believe In,* p. 70)

An excellent resource to consult concerning the process of conversion within evangelization and catechesis can be found in chapter 1 of the *General Directory for Catechesis*. It is important to recognize that universal Church documents have repeatedly called the Church to model its faith-formation programs on the catechu-menal process. One of the primary reasons for this is that the cate-chumenal process explicitly fosters and incorporates the first step of Christian discipleship.

Step Two: Faith Practices

Once a person has been captivated by the Gospel, he or she is ready to enter into an apprenticing relationship with a master. The person naturally wants to learn more about what captivates him or her. A master teaches the disciple the Christian way of life and provides (or perhaps helps him or her recognize) a new identity. An appren-ticeship that is successful ends with the apprentice becoming a mas-ter, much like what Pope Paul VI writes: "The person who has been evangelized goes on to evangelize others" (*On Evangelization in the Modern World (Evangelii Nuntiandi),* no. 24). It is important to recog-nize that an apprentice must work hard to master the practices of Christian life.

What Are Faith Practices?

Much work has been done recently in the area of Christian faith practices. Dorothy Bass and Don Richter define *Christian prac-tices* this way in *Way to Live Leader's Guide:*

> Christian practices are not simply healthy attitudes, life skills, or ways of being nice (although these could be part of a given practice). Christian practices go beyond this. They involve us in the activities of God and link us to other practitioners in the past, the present, and the future. Christian practices invite us into Christ's radical way of being in the world. They frequently involve resisting how things are ordinarily done in our culture. A Christian practice is a set of activities Christian people do to-gether over time to address fundamental human needs in the light of and in response to God's active presence for the life of the world in Jesus Christ. (P. 10)

The authors are saying that Christian practice is an activity. Chris-tianity is lived. It is a way of life. The definition also suggests that a Christian practice is learned by doing it with others. Christian prac-tices can never be learned in isolation from the community of faith. The implication is that a disciple needs a master or masters to teach her or him the Christian practice. We are also reminded that all faith practices are responses to Christ and that faith practices engage young people in the mission of the Church. Bass and Richter also make the following main points about each Christian practice:

- It involves us in God's activities in the world and reflects God's grace and love
- It is done together. Those with whom we practice include people we know personally, those around the world, and many people who have come before us or who will come after us. Even when someone is participating in a practice alone, he or she is embraced by this community, which has Jesus at its heart.
- It is learned with and from other people. Almost always, other people have helped us to hear Jesus' invitation and to learn the moves that make it possible to respond. Someone has shared Christ's love with us by making a specific practice a living reality: for example, by welcoming us, by teaching us to make music, or by offering us forgiveness. As we take up our own parts in these practices, we will in turn invite others to join in too.
- It comes to us from the past and will be shaped by us for the future. Our challenge and privilege are to join in each practice where we are. Often it is not completely clear how to do this, however. So we reflect, drawing on the wisdom of the past (including Scripture and history) and being creative as we put the practice into play in our own situation, mindful that what we do will have an influence on generations to come
- It addresses fundamental human needs. Each practice addresses one or more needs that are basic to who we are as human beings created in God's image and offered new life in Christ. When thinking about a practice, it is often helpful to reflect on what really basic part of our humanness is at stake in this practice
- It is thought-full; it relies on beliefs and develops in us certain kinds of wisdom. Christian practices are active and embodied, but that does not mean that they don't involve our minds! They do. The biblical Story clothes each practice with images and words. In addition, each practice relies on

specific Christian beliefs; for example, the belief in the death and resurrection of Jesus Christ gives us hope (grieving) and allows us to repair torn relationships (forgiveness). However, belief doesn't always come before practice: being members of communities where the Christian practices are really lived can help us to understand and embrace the central beliefs of Christian faith more fully.

- It is done within the Church, in the public realm, in daily work, and at home. A Christian practice is not something we do only at church. Each practice takes shape also in the area of social justice, at home, at school, at work, and as a dimension of personal spirituality. Christian practices overlap with the practices of other religious groups at many points, though not in every way.

- It shapes the people who participate in the practice as individuals and as communities. When we live Christian practices, we express who we most truly are: beloved children of God. When we live Christian practices, we also learn to see everyone else as a beloved child of God.

- It comes to focus in worship. Every Christian worship service involves some practicing of the practices, and a full service that includes Holy Communion gives a taste of all the *Way to Live* practices. When we worship, we gather up our whole way to live and offer it to God. At the same time, we are prepared to go out once again into a way to live that is deeply shaped by our worshipful encounter with God.

- It is a strand in a whole way of life. Taken all together, Christian practices add up to a way to live.

(Pp. 10–11)

A young person can participate in a practice such as hospitality through warm acts of welcome, even without comprehending the biblical stories and theological foundations that encourage this practice. At the same time, practices are not only behaviors. It is important to note that within a practice, thinking and doing are inextricably knit together. For example, young people who offer hospitality come to know themselves, others, and God in a different way, and they develop virtues and dispositions consistent with that practice.

A practice is small enough that it can be identified and discussed as one element within an entire way of life. But a practice is also big enough to appear in many different spheres of life. For example, the practice of hospitality has dimensions that emerge as (1) a matter of public policy; (2) something you do at home with friends, family, and guests; (3) a radical path of discipleship; (4) a part of the liturgy; (5) a movement of the innermost self toward or away from others; (6) a theme in Christian theology; and probably much more. Ministry leaders can develop faith practices by doing the following:

- becoming aware of how young people already engage in each practice
- understanding how involvement in each practice draws young people into God's intentions for them and for the world
- creating practical suggestions that young people can pursue in everyday life
- identifying links to the practices in films, books, music, and other areas of culture
- linking adult mentors to teens with a focus on a practice of importance to both and equipping them with a "toolbox" that includes discussion questions, activity suggestions, and a request to share what they have learned about the practice with others
- linking with service opportunities and holding discussions or other explorations during youth and family gatherings
- interweaving active involvement in a practice with times of contemplation and prayer
- focusing a weekend retreat on faith practices

Organizing

Apprenticeships in faith practices of adolescent Christian disciples can be organized in a number of ways. Bass and Richter suggest eighteen "practices," which include story, bodies, stuff, food, creation, creativity, work, play, time, truth, choices, friends, welcome, forgiveness, justice, grieving, music, and prayer (see *www.waytolive. org*).

Another approach is a simplified plan organized around the four traditional forms of catechetical ministry: word, worship, community, and service and justice. Apprenticing young people in the faith practices associated with the ministry of the word includes learning and living the teachings of Christ and the Church. Worship practices engage young people in individual and communal practices of prayer. Community practices mean learning and living the practices of belonging to the Church. Service and justice practices challenge young people to participate in the mission of the Church in the world.

A positive aspect of this approach is that it affirms the strengths of a parish or school in the areas where it is already effectively apprenticing youth and adults in faith practices. Some parishes and schools are excellent at apprenticing young people in the faith practices associated with the ministry of service and justice, while other parishes and schools are excellent in apprenticing youth and adults in the ministry of worship. The fourfold approach of organizing faith practices around the ministry of the word, worship, community, and service and justice can help parishes and schools, and particularly ministry coordinators, think more systematically about apprenticing young people.

Step Three: Disciples on Mission

Who are the masters who can apprentice young people in Christian practices?

That is a challenging question. Most of us would likely say that we could not be considered a master at apprenticing young people in the Christian life. It is likely that Jesus's disciples felt the same way. It was only through the power of the Holy Spirit that the disciples started to "act." That is a good lesson to remember.

There are three masters who apprentice young people in Christian discipleship. The first and primary master is Christ himself. Christ has a way of calling people and captivating them with the Good News in a variety of ways. The secondary masters are the parents of the youth and the parish and school community itself. Both the parents and the faith community are representatives of Christ, so the apprenticing of young people always witnesses to Christ. There is, in effect, only one master: Christ.

Apprentices can eventually become masters. Christian disciples become masters when they have been systematically apprenticed in the knowledge and skills of Christian living and start participating in the transforming mission of the Church. According to John's

Gospel, Jesus tells the disciples in his farewell discourse that they will "do the works that I do and, in fact, will do greater works than these" (14:12). A mature Christian disciple participates in the works of the master. Aaron Milavec makes an interesting distinction between a mature and an immature disciple:

> There is no adequate way for a disciple to gauge the divine power of his/her master save by becoming a participant in that power through a systematic apprenticeship. The mature disciple knows the spiritual power of his/her master by personal participation. The beginning disciples, meanwhile, can only conjecture and romanticize. As the immature lover who is rapt in infatuation, this disciple only relishes and tastes his/her own projections upon the master. Any master who is surrounded with only infatuated adherents is doomed to a quick end. Infatuation dies easily. (*To Empower as Jesus Did*, pp. 141–142)

Milavec also identifies two important processes at work within systematic apprenticeships that form mature disciples: "The first process insures that apprentices assimilate for themselves the settled instincts and performative skills which characterize the living masters of the tradition" (p. 3). This process insures that the tradition is being faithfully handed down. The second process has "masters dedicate their energies to revealing as-yet-undisclosed manifestations of those realities which they serve" (p. 3). The mature disciple faithfully represents the tradition and faithfully keeps the tradition growing and new. Perhaps the heart of this mastery is the personal integration of Christ's love to the extent that it becomes vibrant, captivating, and transforming for both individuals and social structures.

Conclusion

The Church needs now more than ever to utilize an apprenticing process to empower youth and adults to live as disciples of Jesus Christ in the world today. That is basically what Catholic Church documents have been saying for thirty years. It is what the New Testament described two thousand years ago.

Chapter Questions

1. How might youth ministry be different if it was viewed as an apprenticeship?
2. How differently would a parish or school youth ministry look if it operated its ministry as an apprenticeship for youth and adults in Christian practices?
3. What are your parish or school strengths and areas of growth in forming faith practices in the areas of word, worship, community, and service and justice?
4. Who are the Christian masters in your faith community? How might your youth ministry engage those masters in apprenticing adolescent Christian disciples?

Chapter 5

Youth Ministry: The Component of Advocacy

Maggie McCarty

Introduction

In the 1997 United States Conference of Catholic Bishops' document *Renewing the Vision,* advocacy is the first of eight components that "provide a framework for the Catholic community to *respond* to the needs of young people and to *involve* young people in sharing their unique gifts with the larger community" (p. 26). The ministry of advocacy looks not only at the Church structures and practices to more fully integrate youth into the life of the Church but also to the community at large and speaks out against societal ills that threaten the physical and emotional well-being of adolescents and families. The ministry of advocacy calls all people to stand with and for youth in the public arena (in favor of life, education, housing, employment, and other issues). It calls all to empower young people to speak for themselves on issues that affect them (by giving them leadership training and organizational skills), and it calls ministry leaders to develop partnerships with others who will work for communitywide solutions that help put children and families first.

Objectives

This chapter explores advocacy as an essential component of a comprehensive and life-changing Catholic youth ministry, provides a basic understanding of advocacy, and offers practical strategies of advocacy within the congregation and the community at large.

On Behalf of the Young

The 1989 United Nations Convention on the Rights of the Child made it clear that participation is a substantive right of all young people. The demand for recognition of the right of young people to be heard and have an active role in promoting their best interests is far from universally respected, however. Such a demand for recognition represents a significant challenge of the traditional attitudes toward young people in many communities, which often assumes adults are superior decision makers who can represent the best interests of the young.

When the voice of youth is engaged in churches, communities, schools, and organizations, young people grow more capable. They enhance their academic skills with "real world" experience, learning leadership and citizenship skills and the importance of helping and working for and with others.

Just as important, adults grow more energized, creative, and insightful. Their work becomes more responsive, and their hearts become more engaged. Sharing the responsibility of community building lifts the weight of working alone. In our communities young people must be viewed as problem solvers rather than problem makers.

All those involved in ministry have the opportunity to be advocates for and with the young by taking on their causes and positioning themselves to speak on behalf of, and in solidarity with, today's youth.

Advocacy in Youth Ministry

Compared to other components of youth ministry in which youth are gathered, most advocacy happens behind the scenes as leaders build relationships and promote collaboration. Advocacy for youth and their families demonstrates a commitment to stand with those who are most in need in our neighborhoods and in society. In *Renewing the Vision,* parishes are challenged to examine their policies, programs, and ministry initiatives to make sure that youth are considered and included: "The ministry of advocacy engages the Church to examine its priorities and practices to determine how well young people are integrated into the life, mission, and work of the Catholic community" (p. 27).

We advocate for youth when we speak for them and when we give them a voice to speak for themselves. From a practical standpoint, this may mean that when the parish is planning the annual budget for staffing, for buildings, or for a program, youth's concerns are considered. Youth ministry leaders advocate for young people by working together with other leaders and by communicating a vision for youth in the parish community and beyond. Ministry leaders must also help the parish as a whole and the community at large become more youth friendly by enlisting the community's commitment to welcome and value youth.

Advocacy for youth also means looking at all the leadership and decision-making groups in the parish, schools, community organizations, government agencies, and so forth to see who can speak for youth among those leaders. Sometimes the youth ministry coordinator or ministry leaders and volunteers will be the advocate. In other cases youth can be included in leadership groups and can speak on their own behalf.

The ministry of advocacy is not just one function. It cannot be defined with just one activity. Rather, the ministry of advocacy is a posture or mindset that calls all ministry leaders (if not the entire community) to be "for" young people. In that regard advocacy is a process that involves the coordinated efforts of people in changing existing practices, ideas, and distributions of power and resources that affect young people. Advocacy is about both changing specific decisions affecting young people's lives and changing the decision-making process into a more inclusive process. The ministry of advocacy includes these practices:

- affirming and protecting the sanctity of human life as a gift from God and building societal respect for those who most need protection and support—the unborn, the poor, the disadvantaged, the sick, and the elderly
- standing with and speaking on behalf of young people and their families on public issues that affect their lives, such as support for education, quality housing, employment opportunities, access to health care, safe neighborhoods, and the availability of meaningful community activities and services
  . . .
- empowering young people by giving them a voice and calling them to responsibility and accountability around the issues that affect them and their future (This involves education, leadership training, skills building, and organization to mobilize young people for action.)

- developing partnerships and initiatives with leaders and concerned citizens from all sectors of the community to develop a shared vision and practical strategies for building a healthy community

(Renewing the Vision, pp. 27–28)

Guiding Principles of Youth Advocacy

Invest in Youth

Ministry leaders must advocate for young people from all walks of life, from gang members to honor students, fostering recognition of the important role each young person plays in the faith community and in the community at large. The call to invest in youth is predicated on two beliefs—first, that youth are leaders of today, not just tomorrow; second, that healthy young people cannot exist disconnected from their community, and a healthy community cannot exist without meaningful contributions from its youth members. All young people should play a direct role in their own development, ensuring that the policies and institutions that impact them and their communities are accountable to all members of society.

Respect Youth

Ministry leaders must meet young people where they are by respecting youth culture, life experiences, and community relationships. Advocates can also demonstrate their respect for young people by creating an open and safe environment for them to share personal frustrations and life experiences. Advocates often spend time walking the halls of local high schools and detention centers, meeting with guidance counselors, teachers, or probation officers. Advocates get to know young people's parents and extended family. Relationships with young people extend beyond weekly ministry meetings, trainings, or rallies and into neighborhoods where advocates can develop a strong knowledge of the community—the values, traditions, and daily struggles that shape young people's lives.

Include Education

Political education and movement history are powerful tools for mobilizing, educating, and inspiring youth. Advocacy includes the study and discussion of race, class, gender, and sexual identity as a way to connect with young people. In an effort to better understand the conditions young people face, advocates encourage them to discuss their experiences and recognize the individual and collective impact of systemic discrimination—racism, sexism, homophobia, nationalism (anti-immigrant sentiments), and so on.

Promote Youth-Adult Partnerships

Advocates work *with* young people, not *for* them. Respecting youth leadership is a precursor to providing young people with the skills to navigate their lives and engage in collective action. In the ministry of advocacy, adults encourage youth in the development and exercise of their own leadership. In addition, adults provide support, access to resources, and mechanisms for accountability. With adult guidance young people assume control of and responsibility for their own individual and organizational decisions, both good and bad. In all instances youth are able to express ideas, receive feedback, and reflect and refine with peers and supportive adults.

Advocacy Within the Congregation

Youth Minister as Advocate

An advocate is "a person who speaks or writes in support of something, or to be in favor of" (*Webster's New World Dictionary*, s.v. "advocate"). Tracing the word back to its Latin roots, the term means "to call to one's side." The word *advocate* has also been used to mean defense attorney, or spokesperson, mediator, intercessor, comforter, and consoler. From such definitions, we can conclude that an advocate for youth is a person who stands for and with young people.

Advocates develop their vision and ideas and put their words into actions to create positive change that improves young people's lives. Ministry leaders advocate for young people in a number of ways, including these:

- respecting and valuing the opinions of others no matter how old they are
- appreciating the energy and insights of young people
- working *with* youth, not *for* them
- letting go of the role of leader to share power and responsibilities with others, especially the young
- assessing personally held stereotypes, judgments, and preconceptions of young people
- providing young people with the information, training, and support they need to succeed
- not blaming all young people for the actions of one young person
- scheduling meetings at times when youth can participate
- planning for interactive activities that break through tension and age barriers
- planning meaningful and challenging opportunities for youth and adults to serve in the community
- offering moral support and encouragement to young people
- supporting community organizations that involve young people in meaningful roles
- listening to young people express their concerns and perspectives about community issues and helping them take action
- advocating for youth by making sure they're at the table when a group of adults is holding a discussion about them
- connecting with other adult allies
- talking with others about the importance of having a community vision for community youth development

An advocate ensures that the Church and all of society are respectful and inclusive of the life, dignity, and rights of teenagers and their families.

Pastoral Ministries

Every parish has a variety of pastoral ministries: visits to sick people, social-justice committees, food baskets, and so forth. Among the ways to advocate on behalf of youth is to ensure that they are integrated into already existing committees, activities, and events, rather than creating parallel structures in the youth and adult communities. This form of advocacy promotes the gifts of young people and allows their gifts to be shared with the wider community. It also adds an intergenerational component to ministry programming. Instead of youth planning their own mission trip or work-camp experience, ministry leaders must consider creating joint or intergenerational service and mission trips. Instead of young people serving in soup kitchens as a youth activity, ministry leaders must strive to have youth join the parish's social-concerns ministry.

Leadership Ministries

Most parishes have a representative structure, such as a parish or pastoral council. The ministry of advocacy can become concrete by having a member who represents youth ministry (either a young person or a member of the youth ministry team). Advocacy can also happen by offering reports on youth activities and advocating for just wages for youth ministry staff. Young people can speak to the parish council and parish committees on the impact of the youth program on their faith formation.

Liturgical Ministries

Emphasis must be placed on integrating young people into the worshiping life of the community. Full, conscious, and active participation in the parish liturgical life, rather than token or segregated involvement, is integral to fostering the communal faith identity of young people. Ministry leaders must advocate for the participation of young people in all liturgical ministries. Young people need to be visible and present not only at regular Sunday liturgies but also during special feasts and holy days, including Holy Week.

Sunday worship can also be used to celebrate young people in general or to pray for special events in the lives of youth. Special youth-focused Masses such as the annual World Youth Day Mass, a

Mass that celebrates the beginning or the end of the religious education year, or a baccalaureate Mass honoring graduates are excellent ways to advocate for youth. Including important "youth" events, such as exam times, prom season, the end of school, and so forth, in the Prayers of the Faithful not only invites adults to pray for youth but also draws young people into the liturgical experience.

Education and Faith Formation

Parishes traditionally divide their faith-formation experiences by age-groups. Although this model ensures age appropriateness in the larger sense, by the time young people reach their teen years, their spiritual and faith-formation needs become extremely broad. Many teens are ready and willing to delve deeper into their faith, and should be given the option of participating in "adult" formation experiences such as parishwide Bible study and faith-sharing experiences. Motivated teens will self-select those activities when they are ready, and should be invited to attend as well as plan such activities with and for the parish at large.

Communications

Communicating with the parish at large is an important advocacy activity for anyone working in youth ministry. The savvy ministry leader can use several mechanisms to achieve that result. Bulletin boards that are visible, vibrant, and up to date can be an excellent way for the parish to be aware of what is happening with young people. If the parish has a Web site, it too can be used to promote the work and activities of youth. Promoting youth ministry and advocating for young people can happen via newsletters, bulletin announcements, mailings sent to families, parish registration packets, and other broader vehicles that the parish uses to communicate with parishioners. Some parishes use their bulletin each week to highlight the activities of young people. Those bulletins can be used to announce upcoming activities and to highlight youth's accomplishments (such as receiving awards at school or in the community).

Advocacy with the Community at Large

Decisions affecting children and youth are being made at more far-reaching levels than the congregation or school boundaries, and include businesses, human-services agencies, health-care organizations, civic associations, governmental agencies, and others. As individuals, Catholics are called to ongoing participation in public life and to helping shape public policies that reflect their values. Parishes and other Church organizations also participate in public life by applying Catholic social teaching to key issues facing their communities, the nation, and the world, and by speaking out on the moral and ethical dimensions of those issues:

> As a Church we need to provide strong moral leadership; to stand up for adolescents, especially those who are voiceless and powerless in society. We call upon all ministry leaders and faith communities to use the resources of our faith community, the resources and talents of all our people, and the opportunities of this democracy to shape a society more respectful of the life, dignity, and rights of adolescents and their families. (*Renewing the Vision*, p. 27)

Advocacy in the larger community is geared to improving the lives and participation of marginalized young people and families and to forging broad alliances for reform across society. This type of advocacy is often referred to as citizen-centered, transformative, people-centered, participatory, or social-justice advocacy.

If ministry leaders choose to become involved in advocating for youth in the broader community, these simple approaches should be considered:

- Attend a meeting of a group that is already working on the issue of interest.
- Establish or join a coalition of interested individuals and organizations that have common goals.
- Request that legislators or their staff meet to discuss concerns about policies or to reinforce support of policies.
- Write letters to local, state, or national legislators.

- Personalize an issue by collecting stories of particular people who are affected by the cause or issue.
- Invite legislators or their staff to visit the organization or programming to see the issue in action.
- Organize an event to promote the issue to a wider audience (and attract media attention).
- Write a letter to the editor of the local newspaper or an op-ed piece to express an opinion—and encourage others to do the same.

(Adapted from "Ideas for Simple and Not So Simple Advocacy Strategies," in *Working for Change*, September 1995)

Advocacy in the Political Arena

Although the Catholic Church often speaks to issues that are both moral and political, it directs its attention to the issues, not to political parties or candidates.

All activities of the Church (and its parishes, schools, and affiliated organizations) in the political arena must conform to the requirements of section 501(c)(3) of the Internal Revenue Code, which prohibits tax-exempt organizations from participating or intervening in political campaigns on behalf of or in opposition to any candidate for public office.

As a result Church organizations, as well as individuals as representatives of Church organizations, are prohibited from engaging in partisan political activities, including raising money for candidates or political parties, making or distributing statements favoring or opposing candidates or parties, running for elected office, or otherwise participating in political campaigns.

Church employees and officials, however, including clergy and religious, acting in their individual capacity as private citizens, may participate freely in the political process, provided they are not acting as representatives of Church organizations or utilizing Church facilities or assets. At times it may be difficult to distinguish between activities undertaken as a private citizen and activities undertaken as a Church representative, and prudence should be exercised in that regard.

Permissible Activities

- endorsing or opposing legislation, including ballot referenda
- distributing bulletin inserts on moral issues and on the moral responsibilities of voters
- providing educational materials on public policy issues, but not on candidates
- arranging for groups to meet with their elected officials to advocate for or against legislation
- encouraging letter writing, phone calls, and other contacts with candidates and elected officials about issues
- inviting all candidates for public office to a church-sponsored public forum, debate, or candidates' night
- conducting a nonpartisan voter registration drive on church property
- distributing unbiased candidate questionnaires or voting records on a wide variety of issues

Prohibited Church Activities

- endorsing or opposing candidates for political office
- distributing bulletin inserts regarding specific candidates
- distributing or permitting distribution of partisan campaign literature under church auspices or on church property
- arranging for groups to work for a candidate for public office
- funding or financially supporting any candidate, political action committee, or political party
- inviting only selected candidates to address your church-sponsored group, or permitting or hosting political meetings on church property
- conducting voter registration that is slanted toward one party
- rating candidates numerically, or "favorably" and "unfavorably"
- sharing parish resources, including mailing lists, with political campaigns or parties

These lists serve as a summary of the principle "do's and don'ts" of political activity for tax-exempt organizations. More detailed information on the guidelines can be obtained from the United States Conference of Catholic Bishops.

Identifying Processes for Advocacy

A lasting solution needs to get to the root causes of a problem. Problems have many causes and many possible solutions. Advocacy strategies attempt to solve a problem step by step by getting at its systemic causes and focusing on specific issues.

The following process can help, regardless of whether advocacy is to take place at a parish or school or on a state or national level.

Analysis involves exploring the origins and systemic causes of social and political problems. Analysis can encompass issues of personal identity—gender and sexual orientation, for example—as well as broader community issues of poverty and racism. In many cases advocacy helps young people unravel the personal and the political, allowing them to understand their personal struggles in broader social and political contexts. Analysis entails transforming a problem into an issue and identifying parties responsible for bringing about desired changes. Analysis builds skills such as researching, planning, critical thinking, strategy development, debate, consensus building, and discussion.

The following questions can help guide ministry leaders in the process of analysis:

- What is the situation that calls for involvement?
- Whose voice needs to be heard (youth, youth advocate, parent, and so forth)?
- What message needs to be heard? What goals are be to achieved through actions?
- Who needs to hear the voices?
- Are there other voices that can join together?

Action involves a collective, public activity that confronts decision makers and pressures them to make a desired change. Action often begins by recruiting allies and members and engaging in community education. Action includes a range of activities: speaking at parish council meetings, writing letters to officials, circulating petitions, displaying banners, and holding public demonstrations. Action also helps young people build relationships, develop a sense of life purpose, and contribute to their community in meaningful ways. Action helps young people see their communities as places of possibility and change.

Reflection is an important component of advocacy because it fosters personal, intellectual, and spiritual growth. Participants learn to evaluate their strategies, monitor their activities, and even gauge their own commitment to changing a problem. Reflection can also deepen critical-thinking skills as participants explore new solutions and cultivate new allies. Reflection might include journaling, debriefing with peers about an issue or an experience, or discussing the effectiveness of a particular event. As an advocacy strategy, reflection yields insight and "lessons learned" about experiences that can be applied to other areas of young people's lives.

More specifically, reflection yields at least three important outcomes. First, it fosters a sense of commitment. Young people come to realize their role in fostering change in their communities, and with this knowledge, gain a sense of civic responsibility. Over time this ability to make commitments translates into other areas of young people's lives—family, relationships, school, and career.

Second, reflection builds young people's identities at a critical developmental stage, fostering a sense of hope and agency. New experiences and opportunities encourage young people to apply those characteristics in other areas of their lives.

Third, reflection helps young people heal from harmful social and personal experiences by creating emotional and spiritual wellness. Through support groups, prayer services, group discussions, and gatherings, young people develop psychological, physical, emotional, and spiritual wellness.

Conclusion

The ministry of advocacy helps place young people behind the microphone at city council meetings, on parish commissions, and in door-to-door conversations with their neighbors as they work toward community change. By being present and active within the faith community and the community at large, youth demonstrate their capacity to function as community assets and achieve real improvements in the life of the community. As young people assume a more prominent role in parish ministry, there is potential for cascading influence: as young people assert their voices in public discourse, the needs of young people get incorporated into a broader community agenda. Advocacy helps to generate a respect for youth and their issues among parishioners, business owners, Church leaders, elected officials, policy makers, and key community leaders. The ultimate impact of advocacy is both simple and profound: the engagement of large numbers of young people in leading successful efforts for positive community and systemic change.

Chapter Questions

1. How are the voices of young people honored and heard in your parish community? in the larger community?
2. What has been your richest experience of working with others (collaborating) or on behalf of others (as their advocate)?
3. In what way are the gifts, talents, and energy of young people respected and utilized within your parish community? within the larger community?
4. What type of skills, knowledge, supports, and opportunities do young people need to transform social and community problems? How does young people's participation in addressing those issues prepare them for productive adulthood?

Chapter 6

Youth Ministry: The Component of Catechesis

Terri Telepak with Barbara A. Murray

Introduction

The United States Conference of Catholic Bishops' primary document on youth ministry, *Renewing the Vision,* states that effective catechetical ministry "helps adolescents *develop* a deeper relationship with Jesus Christ and the Christian community, and *increase* their knowledge of the core content of the Catholic faith. The ministry of Catechesis also helps young people *enrich* and *expand* their understanding of the Scriptures and sacred tradition and their application to life today, and *live* more faithfully as disciples of Jesus Christ" (p. 29).

By engaging young people in a systematic study of the Scriptures and Catholic doctrine, involving them in prayer and worship, and fostering their participation in justice and service, our efforts will help them take their rightful place as young disciples for the Reign of God.

Objectives

This chapter identifies the aims and foundations of adolescent catechesis, communicates an understanding of catechesis in the context of the tasks of the *General Directory for Catechesis,* and illustrates the comprehensive relationship between adolescent catechesis and youth ministry.

The Aim of Adolescent Catechesis

Effective adolescent catechesis engages young people in an ever-deepening understanding of the person of Jesus and assists them in applying his teachings to their lives. "Faith is a personal encounter with Jesus Christ, making of oneself a disciple of him" (*General Directory for Catechesis,* no. 53). The aim of adolescent catechesis, therefore, is to deepen young people's relationship to Jesus; strengthen their identity as Catholics; empower their understanding of Catholic

Tradition, doctrine, and the sacred Scriptures; and engage them in discipleship.

Adolescents are naturally curious, and they seek to understand the world and their faith. Ministry leaders who provide opportunities to relate the Scriptures, Church Tradition, and magisterial teaching to the lived experiences of young people help them grow in their understanding of Catholic teaching and assist them in articulating that understanding. By engaging the *minds* of the young, the catechist invites them into the act of believing.

Catechesis deepens adolescent faith by leading young people to recognize and reverence the sacred among them. Young people are invited to open themselves to receive and to deepen their relationship with God. The ministry of catechesis helps young people respond to God's freely given grace. By engaging the *hearts* of the young, catechesis becomes an activity of trusting.

Faith challenges young people to walk in the footsteps of Jesus, and catechetical ministry transports them to places and sites where they encounter the presence of Christ. Catechesis exposes young people to moments that can transform them from fledgling apprentices into passionate disciples, giving them the knowledge and tools for living lives of faith. Catechesis helps young people understand the importance and the consequences of the teachings of the Church and how those teachings affect their lives and their actions. Catechesis engages the *hands* of the young because it calls forth a response to the Gospel message, especially the Great Commandments.

The Focus of Adolescent Catechesis

Rooted in Jesus Christ

Effective catechesis with adolescents helps them understand how to answer the question Jesus put to his disciples: "Who do you say that I am?" (Matthew 16:15). It guides them, through reflection on the death, life, and Resurrection of Jesus, to an understanding of Jesus as the Incarnate Word of God.

Further, adolescent catechesis invites young people to explore a personal relationship with Jesus so that they may grow in their understanding and knowledge of his teachings and the passions and commitments that framed his life.

Anchored in the Developing Human Person

The roots of effective catechesis with adolescents must be strengthened and anchored in an understanding of the developing human person. For adolescents to appropriate and integrate faith, catechetical efforts must be responsive to their distinctive needs, interests, and concerns. Catechetical learning experiences should focus on a variety of learning styles (visual, auditory, participatory), address the lived experience of the learner, and inform participants in a way that honors their developmental stages of learning.

Nourished by the Church's Mission

"The Church 'exists in order to evangelize.'[5] . . . Evangelization must be viewed as the process by which the Church, moved by the Holy Spirit, proclaims and spreads the Gospel throughout the entire world" (*General Directory*, nos. 46 and 48). The ministry of catechesis acknowledges the presence of God already in the lives of young people and provides them with the education and skills necessary for their participation as young evangelizers. Their energy and ideals offer the Good News of Jesus to their peers and to the parish community itself. Catechesis is nourished by the Church's mission when young people enter into a deeper relationship with Jesus and learn to live as disciples who are willing and able to share their gifts with the wider community.

Sustained in Christian Communities

For Catholics, faith is deeply communal, and it is in community that faith is nurtured. "The Christian community is in herself living catechesis. Thus she proclaims, celebrates, works, and remains always a vital, indispensable, and primary *locus* of catechesis" (*General Directory*, no. 141).

The entire community engages in lifelong faith formation, and each part of the community has a responsibility to foster the faith of the others. Recent discussion has termed this "whole community catechesis." A vibrant, spirit-filled community is a critical component of any ministry to and with young people. Each setting of the Christian community offers its own unique charisms and challenges. Adolescent catechesis rooted in Jesus Christ takes form and sustenance from the community, for "Catechesis prepares the Christian to live in community and to participate actively in the life and mission of the Church" (*General Directory*, no. 86).

The Family Community
People's lives and values are first shaped in families. There the young encounter critical experiences that lead them to Jesus Christ and the doctrines of the Church that form a life of discipleship. Those experiences are never forgotten and provide the impetus for lived faith. They include love and forgiveness, fidelity, commitment, compassion, and service. The family is the context in which most young people first learn to pray and to turn to God in times of celebration and crisis. The family, then, becomes the primary religious educator for young people, and the parish communities' efforts to support families will be of benefit to the entire community, both local and global.

The Parish Community
The life of the parish impacts the way it catechizes. A welcoming community that invites people to share their gifts will evangelize, teach, and preach God's word in Jesus. The parish assembles the faithful, leads them in worship and prayer, and invites them to participate fully in the sacraments. The parish is a sign of good news when it intentionally works for peace and justice for all humans, giving preferential treatment to those who are most needy. For young people the parish community provides an assembly of mentors, catechists, heroes, and friends, who care for them, challenge them, and "foster [their] total personal and spiritual growth" (*Renewing the Vision*, p. 15).

The Catholic School Community
Catholic schools provide a unique opportunity to create a respectful and challenging environment that nurtures faith. Schools catechize in the religion classroom, but also in their settings of

communal life based on Catholic values. A Catholic school often offers opportunities for young people to be involved in activities that foster their spiritual growth through campus ministry, school liturgies, and retreat programs. Catholic schools engage young people in the Church's mission in the world as they lead their students in service to others and "develop in the school community an atmosphere animated by a spirit of liberty and charity" (*General Directory*, no. 259).

The Multicultural Community

An important community element is inculturation, a process by which the Church interacts with various cultures, thereby enriching both. Inculturation "is not simply an external adaptation designed to make the Christian message more attractive or superficially decorative. On the contrary it means the penetration of the deepest strata of persons and peoples by the Gospel which touches them deeply, 'going to the very center and roots'[6] of their cultures" (*General Directory*, no. 109).

When young people are given the opportunity to share their own unique cultural heritages (we are not only multicultural in the sense of race, ethnicity, and nationality, but also in terms of gender, class, sexual orientation, able-bodiedness, and age), catechesis is enriched and broadens the learners' concepts of God's activity in the lives of others. Identifying, naming, and claiming the unique cultural markers operative in the day-to-day lives of young people helps them recognize the gifts of arts, fashion, values, rituals, customs, and tradition as part of God's gifts. Effective catechesis also includes the call to transform cultures when aspects of culture are not in harmony with Gospel values.

Tasks for Catechetical Ministry with Adolescents

The *General Directory for Catechesis* names six interrelated tasks for catechetical ministry with adolescents. The goal of the catechetical tasks is to lead young people to a lively faith that is centered in the teachings of Jesus and the mystery of Christ:

- *Promote knowledge of the faith.* In order to give witness to what we believe as Catholics, a knowledge and understanding of both Tradition and Scripture is necessary. (No. 85)
- *Liturgical education.* Worship is the active celebration of the faith community, and catechesis deepens the experience by fostering an understanding of our rituals and their connection with life. (No. 85)
- *Moral formation.* Catechesis empowers young people to live a more faithful Christian life—personally, interpersonally, socially and politically. Furthermore, catechesis seeks to promote critical reflection and interpretation that affirms and critiques the values and behaviors of culture and society. (No. 85)
- *Teaching to pray.* Catechesis fosters both the personal and communal dimension of prayer. Teaching the traditional prayers of the Church and encouraging the opportunities for learning how to pray brings vitality to the faith community. "When catechesis is permeated by a climate of prayer, the assimilation of the entire Christian life reaches its summit." (No. 85)
- *Education for community life.* Catechesis forms disciples for the community, providing the opportunities for responsible participation in the life, work, and mission. Our actions and decisions affect our family, the neighborhood, our friends, school, the parish, and the larger Body of Christ. (No. 86)
- *Missionary initiation.* For adolescents, the missionary setting can be biology class, the basketball game, and the after-school job. The task is to bring Gospel values into the daily lives of young people, no matter the circumstances or the setting. (No. 86)

The Relationship of Adolescent Catechesis and Youth Ministry

An integral relationship exists between comprehensive youth ministry and effective adolescent catechesis. Youth ministry is most comprehensive when it includes a systematic and intentional catechesis, specifically the learning, doing, and reflective processing of faith. An effective catechetical program for adolescents recognizes the need to help young people apply what they have learned to their everyday lives, and youth ministry provides moments to develop skills and practice what is learned.

A good practitioner of youth ministry comprehends that each moment with young people offers catechetical opportunities. The challenge for those in ministry with young people is intentionality. Asking the question, "What makes *this* dance, *this* field trip, and *this* social different from a secular event?" begins to change the dynamics of the gathering. Celebrating feast days in conjunction with a dance is an opportunity to educate youth on the lives of the saints. Preparing a field trip is an opportunity to explore the Church's great tradition of pilgrimage. And preparing for a social with sessions on identifying and including the marginalized is a way to surface the richness of Catholic social teachings. This is youth ministry and catechesis at its fullest.

Renewing the Vision identifies the need to "enter a new stage in its development" (p. 7) as the Church seeks to minister with the young. In order to move into this new stage, the entire faith community becomes an essential part of the development of its youngest members. Catechesis within the context of the faith community welcomes young people and offers them a place where they learn to lead a life of faith, deepen their Catholic identity, practice the faith skills they are learning, and discover support in an important time of their lives. It is within the community that young people learn what it means to be a person of faith.

The Elements of Effective Catechesis

When deciding how to implement catechetical efforts, local leaders need to determine the major thrust of their approach. They need to establish how they will gather young people for programs and how they also might employ nongathered strategies. Ongoing formation in the faith "is accomplished through a great variety of forms: 'systematic and occasional, individual and community, organized and spontaneous'"[7] (*General Directory,* no. 51). Several forms of catechesis require an intentional and planned approach. It is important to note, however, that all catechesis is not intentionally planned or taught in a classroom. Effective ministers are always aware of the teachable moments that present themselves through daily living. The life issues of young people, such as family needs, current events (local and international), health concerns, peer friendships, crisis, and sporting events all provide ample opportunity to connect the real issues of teens with their faith. Those moments of informal catechesis can link theological reflection, the Scriptures, and Church teaching to current and pertinent issues that impact a young person's faith. Intentional and planned catechesis is most successful when used with various learning methods, activities, or approaches. The 2003 study "Effective Youth Ministry Practices in Catholic Parishes" highlights aspects of catechetical programming with adolescents and offers the following important elements to consider:

- Faith development is lifelong and developmentally appropriate.
- Catechesis rests solidly on the teachings of the Church.
- Knowledge of and practical skills for living the Catholic faith are integrated in the teaching and learning experience.
- The culture of the adolescent is respected and informed by the wisdom of faith.
- A variety of learning styles, methods, and activities honors the diversity of young people.
- The learning environment is characterized by warmth, trust, acceptance, and care.
- The family is integral to the faith development of young people.
- Supporting the faith development of the family is essential.
- Acknowledging and including the multicultural gifts of young people enriches everyone.
- Programming approaches are filled with variety.
- It explicitly invites young people to consider their vocational call.

(P. 6)

The findings of research from the study also include these aspects:

- It seeks open-minded, authentic, and faith-filled adult facilitators.
- It includes community building.
- It includes peer sharing, youth witness, and youth leadership.
- It is experiential, active, and innovative.
- It is supported by parish staff, families, and parish communities.
- It is creative in its approach to teaching and learning skills.

(P. 6)

Conclusion

Christ-centered, passionate catechesis is a gift to the young Church among us. It is an essential component of ministry with adolescents and a critical element of their lifelong faith formation. Catechesis engages young people in discipleship that is grounded in the life and mission of the Church. It assists them in understanding who Christ is for them and how they are called to be active and vital members of the Church. It offers a systematic, balanced, and comprehensive sharing of the truths of our faith, and it encourages young people to live grace-filled lives. Catechesis helps them understand that from baptism until death, everyone is called to share in Christ's redemptive work and that it is a lifelong journey. Catechesis helps young people recognize that they will share in that work, and Pope John Paul II challenges them to do so in his XII World Youth Day message, delivered August 1996:

> Jesus' dwelling is wherever a human person is suffering because rights are denied, hopes betrayed, anxieties ignored. . . . As disciples and friends of Jesus, become the agents of dialogue. . . . and the ambassadors of the Messiah you have found, . . . so that many more young people of your age may be able to follow his footsteps; their way lighted by your fraternal charity and by the joy in your eyes that have contemplated Christ. (Nos. 4–5)

Chapter Questions

1. How were you formed as a disciple of Jesus? How did you learn to minister, teach, or lead? Who were your role models? Were you ever in the role of apprentice of the faith as a retreat team leader, catechist, or volunteer? What did you learn from that experience that is still with you?
2. How can you be more aware of or knowledgeable about youth culture? Are you comfortable with varied methods and teaching styles that are age appropriate?
3. How can catechesis go "beyond the classroom"? What's the connection to liturgy, the whole life of the parish, home life, and prayer?
4. The long-term goal for adolescent catechesis is knowledgeable, active adult Catholics. How does the short period of catechesis with adolescents fit into the "whole of life"?

Chapter 7

Youth Ministry:
The Component of Community Life

Barbara A. Murray

Introduction

At the heart of the Scriptures is the consistent call to community. Throughout the sacred texts, we hear the stories of covenant and faithlessness, commitment and betrayal, invitation and challenge, turning from and turning toward. And always at the center of the call is the God who loves beyond measure, the God who is community and who desires all followers to become community, as a sign of God's activity in the world.

Ministry with adolescents is no less a part of God's call to community. *Renewing the Vision* locates community as an essential component of ministry with the young. *Renewing the Vision* points to discipleship, responsible participation, and personal and spiritual growth as the main goals for ministry with young people. Those goals cannot be reached without community. A quick scan of the remaining components highlighted in *Renewing the Vision* also helps us realize that they cannot be achieved in isolation. Community is the very heart and soul of who we are as Catholic Christians. Community is central to the lives of adolescents themselves, and building community among them and within the parish community is the focal point of anyone who ministers with that age-group.

Objectives

This chapter focuses on understanding the scope of community life and its importance for the adolescent, identifies strategies to help young people begin to be connected with the wider faith community, identifies some of the theoretical and pastoral principles of community life, and recognizes questions to help parishes look at their own reality in order to identify ways to foster a more community-centered approach to parish youth ministry.

To Be Community

The Church is a whole community, made up of young and old alike. The following are key questions for those who are in ministry with the young:

- How do we help young people become an active and viable part of the parish community?
- Are the existing models of youth ministry responding well to the needs of the young who belong to the faith community?
- What do we need to do differently in order to involve the entire parish community in the faith development of youth?

Taking a serious look at those questions begins to open and enliven a parish's ministry with its young in a way that brings new life and energy to the entire community. When we respond to the gifts and creativity of young people, we are enriched. When we welcome them as an important part of the community, we are made whole. In the process we move toward the reality of what God is calling forth in our lives, together, for the sake of all humankind.

The goal of community life within the Church is to nurture faith in a way that is particular to the specific community while attending to the truth of the Catholic Church. Each parish will live out its faith in ways unique to the makeup of its members. How that community decides to respond to the needs and growth of its youngest members will be a sign of where that community places its values.

> The attitude of all community members toward its young must be authentic (young people can spot a phony a mile off), positive, and understanding. In addition, what we say and do (or what we don't say or do) communicates volumes to young people. Parish communities and programs that are inviting and supportive and that help young people get to know others and build trusting relationships will be authentic Christian communities. (Ann Marie Eckert, *Total Youth Ministry: Ministry Resources for Community Life,* p. 23)

Renewing the Vision points to the importance of community life in the lives of young people and highlights the goals of building environments, developing relationships, and nurturing Catholic faith as the source of good ministry. In addition, the document points to broadening our understandings beyond not only "*what* we do (activity), but *who* we are (identity) and *how* we interact (relationships)" (p. 34).

Good environments for faith growth are essential to the lives of young people. It is important that youth know their presence is not only accepted by the parish but also desired, because without them the community is not whole. Good parish environments provide safe places for asking hard questions, for sharing experiences, and for experiencing creativity in ways that are life giving for all. Good environments take time to build because they require trust, openness to diversity, recognition of shared Gospel values, and commitment to the journey of faith.

If community life is the core of the faith life, then building relationships is the heart of the community. Faithfulness to this task is hard because we are human and so much of life can impact how we grow to trust one another. It is important, however, for us to be faithful to the journey that grows trust, rooted in the Gospel messages of Jesus. We trust and we believe despite the difficulties we may encounter, because as Christians that is what we are asked to do. Learning to trust and to build relationships mirrors the road to Calvary, where betrayal, denial, and suffering all lead to new life. Jesus has shown us the way.

Opportunities abound within a parish community, and a variety of avenues are available to connect young people with the ongoing life of the parish. List the number of ministries already present in your parish. Now ask yourself how you can connect young people with those ministries and how you can find adults who are willing to mentor them until they are comfortable with what they are asked to contribute. For example, young people are often willing to be lectors but are thrown on the altar without practice and without guidance as to how lectors participate and contribute to the liturgy. Simple acts like when to move to the lectern can be learned. What additional traditions does your community use? Does one bow before the altar and then proceed to the lectern? Has enough practice occurred so the young lector will be able to pause when necessary and speak so that all can hear, with respect and a keen sense of proclamation of the word of God? *From Age to Age: The Challenge of Worship with Adolescents* points to the provision of formation and catechesis for the sake of discipleship. Adults have a responsibility to teach the skills that will help young people be successful as they begin to practice their gifts for the sake of the larger community. Faithful and committed adults can be advocates and mentors for young people as they begin to step into new roles of service with the faith community.

Discipleship and Community

One of the primary tasks of a faith community, if not *the* primary task, is to pass on the faith to the next generation. The task is not simply to pass on the faith but to create "missionaries" who are to share the Good News of Jesus with everyone they meet. Disciples not only share what they know about Jesus but also live out their lives as Jesus did. *Renewing the Vision* draws attention to the task at hand and states clearly that ministry with young people is a "concern for the entire church community, especially for leaders in parishes, schools, and dioceses" (p. 1).

The importance of the formation, education, and spiritual development of the young person is matched by a growing call for attention to the formation, education, and spiritual development of adults who minister with the young. To be effective in passing on the faith, adults must be educated and formed in understanding the importance of the many aspects of ministry with youth. *Renewing the Vision* points parish leadership to a ministerial and pastoral approach with adolescents. Relational, goal-centered, and multidimensional approaches are necessary to touch the lives of the young. Ministry with this age-group is to be holistic and attentive to the developmental needs of the age-group; being people-centered and needs-focused is essential to the vision of a community's response to their youth.

Creating opportunities for young people to gather together is important for building relationships and identifying their needs. Young people have a developmental need to connect with their peers through gathered activities, and they often express their need for community in recreational terms. Their desire for trips, social events, and "fun" is often their way of articulating their need for a sense of community—a sense of belonging.

Equally important are the times when young people gather with the parish community for worship, service, learning, apprenticeship, and catechesis. In addition to gathering for sacramental preparation, it is equally good to gather to celebrate life.

Young people hunger for meaning in their lives. They are passionate about God's activity and what it means for the world. They are creative in recognizing opportunities to serve others, and are in need of communities that allow them to use the gifts they have been given. Service to, with, by, and for young people would take on new meaning if they understood the basic social teachings of the Church and were encouraged to question and explore the teachings in relationship to their service activities. They deserve no less than the best efforts of the community.

The *General Directory for Catechesis* is a significant tool that can be used to develop the minds and hearts of the young for discipleship. It can help youth ministers determine how to evangelize young people in a way that faithfully passes on what the Church teaches. Every moment in ministry with young people is a catechetical moment in that we can discover ways to teach young people what it means to live a Jesus-centered life.

A parish catechetical approach to youth ministry will be invitational, respectful, celebratory, affirming, and focused on the family. The parish will always realize that the goal is to help young people make the connection between their life stories and *the* faith story in a way that is real and relevant.

Young people want to know about their Church. They want to know where the Church stands on life issues, even if they do not fully understand. There is a gift in knowledge that offers security and courage for the journey of discipleship. The parish that takes time to extend the invitation to discipleship and to create and offer tools for the journey is the parish that values not only the young but also the entire community.

Apprenticing young people in discipleship means not only teaching them skills but also helping them understand the truths that support the skills. Young people desire to know core truths, and apprenticing helps them develop knowledge for life. Learning sessions centered on the faith and based in experience help young people surface questions that connect them to the reality of their own lives and what that reality means for their relationship with the broader faith community, both locally and globally. For example, a learning session on justice that helps young people learn the Church's teachings and then enter into the reality of those who "have not" is life changing.

It is important to use images and experiences that are rich with meaning and a sense of awe and wonder in the formation of young people. Again, using the justice session as a model, inviting participants to be in dialogue with those whom the world considers to be poor helps young people comprehend the broad and underlying causes of poverty from the perspective of those who live in poverty.

It is equally important to look at the diversity of the community in order to discover new ways of teaching and learning and sharing: What do immigrants have to tell us about poverty? What do grandparents have to share about what they have learned about poor people? How do we "see" the poor in our midst, and what are their voices telling us? All are examples of ways to explore the diversity of the community.

Exposing young people to the scriptural teachings of Jesus is essential in connecting them to the past and to those who have walked before us. Utilizing the Scriptures to teach young people why justice is important and how it is connected to their lives provides life-changing learning and discipleship.

Practical Strategies

The *General Directory for Catechesis* identifies catechesis as a "community need" and a "community right"[8] and recognizes that the "recipient of catechesis is the whole Christian community and every person in it" (no. 168). That focus is certainly the basis of recent studies and development toward whole-community catechesis, where young people are not separated from the learning environment of the entire parish but are included in ways that are mutually beneficial and life giving. Whole-community catechesis can be discovered in intergenerational prayer, where participants share concerns. The prayers can be experienced using a variety of forms. For instance, having someone from an older generation teach someone from a younger generation how to pray the rosary and why that prayer has been an important part of his or her journey of faith can broaden a young person's understanding of its importance.

Creating opportunities for faith experiences and faith sharing in the context of learning key teachings of the Catholic Church will inform young people and assist them in their process of becoming lifelong Catholics.

Bible study experiences can help a young person comprehend the faith journey of the ancient Israelites and discover how those stories teach about commitment and covenant and why those virtues continue to be important today.

Inviting and encouraging young people to share their love of music and relating that music to Gospel lessons opens opportunities for learning and sharing among different generations. Those times can be important opportunities for young people to share the stirrings of their own hearts, teaching others something important about God's activity in their lives.

It is extremely important for the Christian community to involve its young people in its outreach, not as an isolated "youth group" but together with all members, in order to hear stories, share insights, discover God together, and grow in confidence.

Involving young people in the ongoing liturgical life of the Christian community is another opportunity for catechizing. Regular involvement and participation foster the sense of belonging that is so central to community.

Belonging to a community of faith in a way that encourages, challenges, and supports young people in their faith journey is the goal of the entire community as well as of the young people themselves. The African proverb "It takes a village to raise a child" is certainly a guiding focus for the Church today. No one program, no one minister, no one effort will address the needs of the young. It will take an entire community, young and old alike, committed to contributing a variety of unique gifts and talents, to be in relationship with young people today.

Chapter Questions

1. What tools can be shared in order to help adults touch the hearts of young people with the Good News of Jesus?
2. How can a parish develop ways to assist young people in the development of the skills they will need to become their truest and fullest selves for the sake of the Reign of God?
3. Evaluate current parish ministries and activities that already include young people. What are the strengths? How might those ministries be strengthened?
4. Consider parish ministries and activities that do not include young people. How might young people be invited and welcomed?
5. Identify ways youth ministry programs can be more inclusive of the wider parish community.
6. What opportunities exist for young people to build quality relationships with caring, faith-filled adults?

Chapter 8

Youth Ministry:
The Component of Evangelization

Frank Mercadante

Introduction

In addition to having a wide spectrum of emotional connotations associated with the word *evangelization,* there is often an ambiguity about its meaning and practice. Yet the Church as a whole, and all its members, are called by Christ to be evangelizers, to proclaim the Good News to others, and to transform our society and culture.

Many Catholics still understand evangelizing to be primarily a Protestant activity. Although the word *evangelization* is making a comeback in Catholic vocabulary (thanks to Pope John Paul II and recent Church documents), it's far from the common Catholic vernacular.

Evangelization is nothing less than the lifeblood of the Church, and therefore the heartbeat of Catholic youth ministry. Bridging the gap between recognizing evangelization as a priority and actually practicing it is an essential task for building life-transforming youth ministries.

Objectives

This chapter explores evangelization as an essential component of a comprehensive and life-changing Catholic youth ministry, provides a basic theological understanding of Catholic evangelization, offers practical steps toward developing an evangelistic spirituality in both teens and youth ministry leaders, discusses the concepts and practical implications of the six dynamics of youth evangelization, and provides a concrete understanding of the pastoral implications of an evangelistic youth ministry.

Defining Catholic Evangelization

Jesus's final act on Earth was commissioning his disciples to preach the Gospel to all creation (Mark 16:15). The Church "exists in order to evangelize" (*On Evangelization in the Modern World [Evangelii*

Nuntiandi], no. 14). Furthermore, evangelization is described as the "essential mission"[9] (no. 14) of the Church, the "energizing core" of the life of the Church and all its ministries (*The Challenge of Catholic Youth Evangelization,* p. 3).

The road to an impacting, evangelistic youth ministry is paved by a proper understanding of Catholic evangelization, because parish communities cannot impart to the youth what they do not possess. Many of the negative connotations of and hesitancies toward evangelization can be shed with a clearer grasp of the term and practice.

In the original Greek, the word *evangelization* meant "the announcing of good news." To evangelize meant to share positive information with others, like that of a town wedding or an important local athletic victory. In the New Testament, the word carried distinct spiritual implications and was used to describe the activity of sharing the Good News of God's Kingdom.

In a basic sense, at this time in history, evangelization means to share one's faith in Jesus Christ (both through word and example). Ultimately, the purpose of evangelization is to bring about interior change, or conversion, that is lived in an ongoing manner through Christian discipleship. This metanoia, or transformation, is not limited to individual impact; it also has the power to collectively change societies and even the systems, values, and priorities of an entire culture. "The fruit of evangelization is changed lives and a changed world—holiness and justice, spirituality and peace" (*"Go and Make Disciples,"* p. 12).

In *Evangelii Nuntiandi,* Pope Paul VI defines *evangelization* as "bringing the Good News into all strata of humanity, and through its influence transforming humanity from within and making it new" (no. 18).

A Catholic understanding of evangelization includes some distinctive elements. First, evangelization is always invitational. It is accomplished in a manner that is respectful of others' dignity and free choice. If evangelization is done in a manipulative, coercive, arrogant, or unloving manner, that methodology is a contradiction to its very message.

Second, evangelization is always operative in the life of a Catholic. It is not a one-time event, but includes both an initial and an ongoing proclamation of the Gospel. As Catholics, we never grow out of the need for ongoing evangelization. For example, the importance of the liturgy of the word testifies to our ongoing need to hear, believe, and apply the Good News of God's Kingdom in our lives. We need ongoing evangelization to be spiritually re-energized and renewed.

Third, evangelization is communal in nature. It's not simply about being evangelized into a personal relationship with God; it's also about being evangelized into a community of believers. Evangelization that results in a "just me and God" spirituality is missing the mark. The communal dimension includes being nurtured and guided by the teaching and Tradition of the Church and utilizing one's gifts to build up the Body of Christ to serve all humanity.

Fourth, evangelization cannot be contained in a single program; it is more a mindset, in which its threads are woven throughout the entire tapestry of parish life. All members—priests, religious, and laity—are called to make evangelization a priority in daily life.

The Need for Catholic Youth Evangelization

Adolescence is one of the most developmentally significant seasons in life for evangelization. Young people begin asking the significant questions of life: Who am I? Why am I here? What's the purpose of life? What do I believe in? What's important? If the Church is not present and personally connected to teens, it will lose the opportunity to address those spiritual hungers with the truth of the Gospel.

Additionally, teens are beginning to value and develop deeper personal relationships. Children play and share activities together. Teenagers share their feelings, values, perspectives, and very selves with one another. For most teenagers nothing is more sacred than friendship. It is precisely during this time that evangelistic youth ministries should offer teens the opportunity to develop a relationship with Jesus Christ and a community of believers.

Evangelistic Spirituality

One of the first and foundational steps to building an evangelistic youth ministry is to foster an evangelistic spirituality in the faith community. Evangelization is as Catholic as the Eucharist, yet it has not been adopted into Catholic spirituality in the same manner. As a result of immigrant heritage and the privatization of faith, many Catholics do not yet share the value and practice of evangelization as an essential expression of what it means to live out their Catholic faith. If we hope to change the world, we must become, as an entire Church, an evangelizing people. The following steps can help develop an evangelistic spirituality in both our adult and teen leaders.

Model, Live, and Illustrate an Evangelistic Spirituality

Before young people will consider the Christian lifestyle, they need to be in regular contact with sincere and loving believers who demonstrate the reality and power of the Christian message. If a leader is not an evangelizer, she or he cannot expect others to be. Leaders should make it a point to share their evangelization stories (how Christ has made a difference in their lives) with fellow youth workers and teen leaders. One's example is always the best teacher.

A Personal, Meaningful, and Real Relationship with Jesus and His Followers

The Apostle Paul revealed his motivation for proclaiming the Gospel when he spoke of being compelled by the love of Christ (see 2 Corinthians 5:14). Being in a meaningful relationship with Jesus and a community of believers is a natural motivation for evangelizing. The richness of that experience compels us to want others to have it for themselves.

By giving teens the vocabulary, the tools, and the communal support to truly know and love Christ, they will naturally want to share their experience with others—and that is evangelization. In today's postmodern world, experience is the vehicle of truth.

People Deeply Matter to God

The Lord was always looking out for the lost. Jesus invested his entire life for the sole benefit of others. His words, actions, and lifestyle demonstrated his deep love and care for all people. His final act of love on Earth—dying on our behalf—was indicative of his entire life.

Jesus Christ loves everyone. He is truly in love with those we can hardly tolerate, let alone like. The people around us—whom we may love and cherish, find difficult or annoying, or not even know exist—are passionately loved by Jesus Christ. We must learn to value people beyond anything else in life and to pass on that value to both adult and teen leaders.

Intentional in Reaching the Unevangelized

Once adult and teen leaders understand the importance of inviting others to hear and experience God's personal love, we must provide ministerial support for their efforts. Too often teens have little programming to which they can bring an outside friend and feel confident that their friend is going to hear the Gospel in a compelling way. Youth ministry should offer programming that articulates the Gospel in a clear and relevant manner, one that teens can use as a springboard for further conversations of faith with their friends. Any youth ministry that wants teens to both value and practice evangelization must offer programming that intentionally proclaims the Gospel. Finally, we should continually encourage teens to invite their friends to the program's events.

Training, Tools, Resources, and Skills to Share Faith

To become an evangelizer, teens need to be trained in how to share their faith interpersonally. Both adult and teen leaders should be equipped to share their faith stories in a manner that concretely illustrates the Good News. Young people should be able to invite others into a new or deeper relationship with Christ and his community of believers. In other words, ministry leaders need to form skilled youth evangelizers who are capable of sharing their faith at any time and who hold one another accountable to Jesus's call to proclaim the Gospel to all creation.

It is true that young people are busier than ever. Sometimes we see their numerous involvements in outside activities as threats to the Church's influence in their lives. In reality, if we enable teens to be everyday evangelizers, their busyness can be more an opportunity than a liability. Instead of spending all their time at Church events, they can be Church to others in school, sports, jobs, hobbies, and so forth.

(This section is adapted from Frank Mercadante, *Make It Real,* pp. 132–148.)

The Dynamics of Evangelization

The Challenge of Catholic Youth Evangelization identifies six elements comprising the evangelization process. Although each element builds successively on the preceding dynamic in theory, the process is not always linear in practicality. Nevertheless, a youth ministry that evangelizes will practically incorporate each of the following dynamics.

Witness

In the marketplace a great product sells itself. Satisfied customers tell others about its quality, reliability, and usefulness. In the same manner, the positive witness, or authentic Christian life, furnishes a concrete illustration of the power and impact of the Gospel. A life that embodies the values of Jesus will provoke intrigue from others. Pope Paul VI said it well in *Evangelii Nuntiandi:* "Through this wordless witness these Christians stir up irresistible questions in the hearts of those who see how they live" (no. 21).

Practically speaking, both adult and teen leaders should understand the importance of their witness. Formation should be offered in the larger Church and in specific youth ministry training that helps promote Christian integrity. The best youth ministries challenge, encourage, and provide the resources to leaders to help them live their faith in a compelling and contagious manner.

In addition to individual witness, developing a positive programmatic, parish, and institutional witness is also important. The parish that demonstrates hospitality, love, and respect toward all will be the kind of witness that draws the interest of outsiders.

Outreach

The dynamic of outreach comprises all the intentional and spontaneous efforts of reaching out to teenagers. That means becoming an authentic missionary by bravely journeying into the world of teenagers and becoming physically present on their turf. Jesus is the model for outreach. Through the Incarnation, Jesus left heaven to enter the world of those he sought to reach. He went from town to town seeking the lost, healing the afflicted, and proclaiming the Good News of God's Reign.

Outreach is always relational in nature. From a practical perspective, it means building a relational connection with teens by attending their events, making contact outside of organized Church programming, and building relationships that authentically earn one the right to be heard. Furthermore, it means targeting teens that might never come to a Church meeting and finding a meeting ground or interest—bringing the Church to them on their turf.

Relational outreach may not necessarily come naturally to many youth workers. Many youth ministry leaders are functioning from a programmatic paradigm; their personal experience of youth ministry or religious education was primarily within the context of a program that centered on content. Moving to a relational paradigm requires great focus, effort, and accountability on the youth ministers' part. Though such a "shift" may be challenging to some ministry leaders, the end result is well worth the effort.

Proclamation

Evangelization is not complete without explicit proclamation of the Good News of Jesus Christ. A young person may be intrigued by a compelling witness and engaged by a caring adult, but it is in the proclamation of the Gospel that the source and energy behind their life and kindness is revealed. Pope Paul VI had this to say:

Nevertheless this always remains insufficient, because even the finest witness will prove ineffective in the long run if it is not explained, justified—what Peter called always having "your answer ready for people who ask you the reason for the hope that you have"[10]—and made explicit by a clear and unequivocal proclamation of the Lord Jesus. The Good News proclaimed by the witness of life sooner or later has to be proclaimed by the word of life. There is no true evangelization if the name, the teaching, the life, the promises, the kingdom, and the mystery of Jesus of Nazareth, the Son of God, are not proclaimed. (*On Evangelization in the Modern World [Evangelii Nuntiandi]*, no. 22)

So what is the good news we are proclaiming? Essentially, the message is the person of Jesus Christ. It is through the life and teaching of Jesus that God communicates how to live. It is through the suffering and death of Jesus that God communicates his love. And it is through the Resurrection of Jesus that God assures us of our own rising from the death of sin and anything that separates us from the love of God.

We are born with the need to be evangelized. Common to humanity is the longing for something more. Whether it's called a God-shaped hole, a soul's ache, or a holy longing, a hunger for God is something people have. Youth experience those hungers in many ways. Some examples include a need for purpose, a sense of loneliness, a desire to be loved, or a thirst to feel valued or significant. The good news is that the Gospel message satisfies those hungers.

Initial evangelization involves understanding the hunger or hungers of those we are evangelizing (by *listening* to the Holy Spirit and those we are seeking to evangelize) and communicating the strand of the Gospel that best addresses that hunger. Jesus modeled this approach (see Luke 19:1–10, John 3:1–21, and John 4:4–26). Jesus did not recite a canned presentation of the Gospel when evangelizing. Instead, he diagnosed a person's need and tailored his message to address it.

When sharing with a teen who is lonely, we may speak of a God who will never leave us or forsake us (see Hebrews 13:5). To another who feels inferior or worthless, we may share that God thought so much of us that he allowed Jesus to die for us (see John 3:16). Another teen may suffer from anxiety and constant worry. We may share with him or her that God cares so deeply about every detail of our lives that he has the hairs on our head numbered (see Luke 12:7).

Proclamation not only involves the presentation of the abstract truth of Gospel but also often includes the sharing of one's own spiritual journey or story. Young people relate to and find truth in stories. Furthermore, our faith stories are easy to identify with and are concrete illustrations of the Gospel's power to change one's life.

Invitation

We may model the Christian life, build genuine relationships with young people, and even enthusiastically share the Gospel. But if we do not explicitly invite teens to share in the Good News, we have neglected an essential dynamic in the evangelization process. At times an invitation may be inappropriate or premature, but to consistently leave it out of the evangelization process is neglectful.

Invitation includes leading young people into a new or deeper relationship with Jesus. Evangelization is Christocentric; that is, the Person of Jesus is central to the evangelization process. Good proclamation leaves young people with questions of how they might personally respond to Jesus's call to them. Evangelistic invitation solicits a response from the listener. That is illustrated after Peter's evangelistic preaching at Pentecost (see Acts 2:37–38).

Peter offered his listeners some concrete steps to conversion. He explicitly provided an invitation about how to respond to the proclamation. We too should give clear invitations to teens on what Jesus is calling them to do. At that point we should be ready to provide concrete guidance on how to meet Jesus or know him more deeply. Our invitation is not only to receive Jesus but also to be welcomed into our faith community. The person of Jesus and his followers come as a package deal. We are evangelized into a relationship with both Jesus and his Church. We need to intentionally and personally invite young people young people to be a part of, and to participate in, the faith community.

Conversion

Conversion begins to turn the focus from the activity of the evangelizer to the actions of the evangelized.

Conversion is a two-step movement consisting of a *no* followed by a *yes*. First, the *no* involves a change of heart or a breaking with the past. It means turning away from our own ways, priorities, values, perspectives, and behaviors through repentance. Second, we say *yes* to God's ways and perspectives. God becomes our meaning, purpose, and goal in life. Interior conversion is evidenced by outward change (see Luke 3:8).

Conversion is ongoing in the life of a Catholic. An initial conversion, or "aha" moment, may be followed by successive conversions that continue the lifelong process of making a person more like Jesus.

The process of conversion is particularly relevant to adolescence, as youth transition from a childhood faith handed to them by their parents to a personal faith they can authentically call their own. Effective youth ministry is all about providing the support of the faith community while nurturing an affiliating faith. Middle school teens benefit greatly by being surrounded by the faith of a strong community. This corresponds with the early adolescent developmental task of belonging. As teens move into middle adolescence, they begin the developmental process of discovering their identity. During that time effective youth ministry allows teens the freedom to question, struggle, and wrestle with their borrowed faith. Being in a positive environment and with people who are accepting, supportive, and able to effectively address the questions of teens during that searching phase of faith development will help move teens toward an owned and personal faith.

Discipleship

The sixth element of the evangelization process is discipleship. Discipleship is all about living out one's conversion in daily life. It includes the process of growing toward greater faith and spiritual maturity, and being equipped and sent out to live the mission of the Church. It is during the discipleship dynamic that evangelization intersects and overlaps with the other youth ministry components such as catechesis, leadership development, and justice and service. It is during this phase that young people transition from spiritual consumer to world-transformer. Teens move from the starting point of evangelization—"Jesus, what can you do for me?"—to "Jesus, what can you do through me?"

The discipleship dynamic can be practically expressed through youth ministry and larger parish offerings such as catechetical programming, faith mentoring, peer ministry, justice and service opportunities, liturgical ministries, and others.

Strategic Youth Evangelization

Evangelization must be intentional and integrated in every aspect of parish youth ministry. "Evangelization is the energizing core of all ministry with adolescents. All of the relationships, ministry components, and programs of comprehensive ministry with adolescents must proclaim the Good News. They must invite young people into a deeper relationship with the Lord Jesus and empower them to live as his disciples" (*Renewing the Vision,* p. 36). Furthermore, the most effective evangelistic youth ministries are situated within a larger parish vision and practice of evangelization.

Where Evangelization Takes Place for Youth

Evangelization can be done environmentally, interpersonally, programmatically, on the church grounds, off the church grounds, and in nongathering ways.

At Parish Gatherings

First, evangelization is communicated through the general environment or atmosphere of a parish. Parishes should be youth friendly by operating with an awareness of how every parish program, activity, or event impacts young people. Teens know by subtle attitudes, words, and actions whether a parish community values and truly cares for them.

Additionally, those offering youth events must seek to create an evangelistic environment by being welcoming, hospitable, and friendly. If teens feel welcomed and wanted and experience a sense of belonging, significant evangelistic inroads are made. Many young people make decisions regarding their Church involvement based solely on how they are treated at youth ministry events.

Beyond Gatherings

Evangelization can also occur in nongathering ways. Examples include youth newsletters, Web sites, DVD or video libraries, books, and e-mail or instant messaging. In today's technological culture, youth will seek information in the format with which they are most comfortable and familiar, and in many cases, that is via the computer.

Outside the Parish Setting

Being where teens are is critical to effective evangelization. Attending sporting events, school activities, and artistic performances are a few examples of relational youth ministry. Making those connections with teens helps open the door to faith sharing and programmatic involvement.

At Parish Youth Gatherings

Gathering events provide a structured avenue for proclaiming the Gospel to teens. That includes liturgical celebrations, small groups, large groups, retreats, prayer services, youth centers, social events, youth conferences, justice and service events, and so forth. Programs or events can be designed with a particular audience in mind. The best evangelistic events address the perceived needs of teens in order to draw their interest. Examples of perceived needs might be to have fun, to build relationships, or to address a topic of interest such as dating and sex. Once those needs are met, the door to addressing unperceived or unarticulated needs, such as the need to know God, is opened.

The Gospel can be proclaimed in many different venues and in many different ways. The eventual goal, however, is to foster conversion in teens by facilitating an authentic encounter with the person of Jesus Christ.

Chapter Questions

1. When you hear the word *evangelization,* what words, images, feelings, or experiences come to mind?
2. How would you define the word *evangelization?* What are some of the Catholic distinctions?
3. In working with teens, do you agree that "evangelization is the essential mission of the Church"? If so why? If not, why not?
4. In your own words, describe each of the six dynamics of evangelization. What are some of the concrete pastoral implications for each dynamic?
5. What are some of the developmental and cultural dynamics that make adolescence a significant season for evangelization?
6. What is an evangelistic spirituality? In what practical ways can we promote the formation of an evangelistic spirituality in Catholic young people?

Chapter 9

Youth Ministry:
The Component of Justice and Service

Tony Tamberino

Introduction

The proclamation and establishment of the Reign of God demands outreach to poor and oppressed people as well as a commitment to work for justice in the world. Throughout the Gospels Jesus points to injustice, hypocrisy, and selfishness, and challenges those who would hear to change their hearts and live in right relationship with God and others. Jesus's first followers, and the Church ever since, have understood that such a mission is part and parcel of true discipleship.

The component of justice and service as outlined in *Renewing the Vision* must be an integral part of any youth ministry that takes the call to discipleship seriously. The first goal in the bishops' document on youth ministry is clear: "To empower young people to live as disciples of Jesus Christ in our world today," and goal two reinforces the call to involve youth in the work of justice as it seeks "to draw young people to responsible participation in the life, mission, and work of the Catholic faith community" (pp. 9–11).

Objectives

This chapter presents a basic understanding of Catholic social teaching and the disciple's call to work for justice and service, discusses the importance of service learning, offers an appreciation of the value of direct service opportunities, delineates the difference between direct service and advocacy or social action and why both are essential in a balanced program, and presents some ideas on establishing justice and service components for parish or school youth ministry.

The Ministry of Justice and Service

When young people are asked to speak of Jesus and his ministry, the discussion can begin in a number of ways. Some young people will begin with a catalog of his miracles, for example, his calming of the storm or the wedding at Cana, where he changed water into wine. Others will focus on his great storytelling and the parables. Still others will immediately speak of his death and Resurrection as the culmination of his work to win our salvation. Rarely, though, will young people, or adults for that matter, speak of Jesus's mission to the poor and his call for justice for the poor and oppressed. Yet consider that early in his ministry, upon returning to his hometown, Jesus declared that the focus of his ministry was "'to bring good news to the poor. / He has sent me to proclaim release to the captives / and recovery of sight to the blind, / to let the oppressed go free, / to proclaim the year of the Lord's favor'" (Luke 4:18–19).

This mission statement of Jesus's, if we can call it that, brings into sharp focus the importance of the Christian ministry of justice and service to those who are in need.

Catholic Social Teaching

To understand the importance of justice and service for youth ministry, one must have a clear understanding of the basics of Catholic social teaching. In recent years the renewed interest in that aspect of Catholic life and teaching has grown exponentially. Institutions of higher learning have introduced courses on the role of the Church to transform the world into God's kingdom of justice and peace. Many parishes across the country and around the world have initiated social-justice committees and social-ministry groups that do everything from running soup kitchens to educating others on the need to work for justice in the community to advocacy for the unborn, homeless people, elderly people, and any group that is ignored or oppressed. Youth ministers on college campuses and in parishes and high schools have developed service opportunities for young people to "get involved" for justice.

In their 1998 document *Sharing Catholic Social Teaching: Challenges and Directions,* the bishops of the United States clearly situate Catholic social teaching in the Judeo-Christian Tradition:

> Catholic social teaching is a central and essential element of our faith. Its roots are in the Hebrew prophets who announced

God's special love for the poor and called God's people to a covenant of love and justice. It is a teaching founded on the life and words of Jesus Christ, who came "to bring glad tidings to the poor . . . liberty to captives . . . recovery of sight to the blind" (Luke 4:18–19), and who identified himself with the "least of these," the hungry and the stranger (Matthew 25:45). (P. 1)

The bishops go on to exhort the Church in America to act on behalf of justice, and reiterate the major themes of Catholic social teaching in order to give clear direction on how the Church today is to respond to the call for a just society.

The Major Themes of Catholic Social Teaching

Though Catholic social teaching is rooted in the Scriptures and can be seen in the witness and ministry of the Church through the centuries, seven themes have emerged in modern times, as outlined by both papal and episcopal documents. For a comprehensive treatment of those, one must refer to the documents themselves. The following reflections are adapted from *Sharing Catholic Social Teaching*, pages 4–6.

The Life and Dignity of the Human Person
From its outset, human life is created by God and is sacred at every stage. Each human person has been created in the image and likeness of God (see Genesis 1:27), and therefore the dignity of the human person lies at the root of all ethical and moral understanding and action.

The Call to Family, Community, and Participation
The human person is a social being by nature and is called to belong, to love, and to be loved. The human family is the most fundamental social institution, and needs to be supported and protected by all segments of society, particularly civil authority. Each person has a right and responsibility to participate in civil society to help promote the common good of all.

The Rights and Responsibilities of All People

Every human person has fundamental rights that can never be lost: the right to life and to those aspects of life required by human dignity, for example, food, shelter, clothing, and so on. Without the recognition of those rights, human dignity cannot be maintained or authentic community established. Corresponding to those basic rights are responsibilities that each person has to family, other people, and society at large.

The Option for the Poor and Vulnerable

It is clear from the teaching and example of Jesus that care for the poor and vulnerable is an essential component of discipleship. The moral goodness of any society can be judged on how its most vulnerable citizens are treated. Particularly since Vatican Council II, the Church has clearly reiterated this constant teaching: we have as Christian disciples a preferential option for the poor and vulnerable, wherever they are.

The Dignity of Work and the Rights of Workers

Human labor is not simply "a way to make a living; it is a form of continuing participation in God's creation" (p. 5). Work, then, by its very nature, commands a particular dignity, and the rights of those who work should be protected by employers and civil authority. One who works should receive a living wage, have the right to organize and own property, and be able to better her or his situation through economic initiative.

Solidarity

Solidarity calls us to recognize that every human person is a child of God, and as such, we are brothers and sisters, part of the one human family. Despite differences between races, nations, or cultures, all people share interdependence with one another and are called to love of neighbor that extends beyond any social boundaries created by human institutions or laws.

Care for God's Creation

Care for God's creation is a basic responsibility of each and every human person. Dominion given by God to human beings at the dawn of creation requires that we care for the earth and protect all the people on the planet. Living in right relationship with God and others demands responsible stewardship as we use the resources of the world and fulfill our vocation to "fill the earth and subdue it" (Genesis 1:28). This mission has obvious "moral and ethical dimensions that cannot be ignored" (p. 6).

It is eminently clear from this brief overview that authentic youth ministry cannot ignore the component of justice and service. By its very nature, faith—in other words, living in relationship with God—has a social dimension to it (see 1 John 4:20–21). The human person is created for relationship, lives and thrives only in relationship, and finds meaning and purpose through relationship with other humans and with God. Authentic Catholic teaching challenges anyone who would follow Christ to move beyond self and take up the vocation to help establish God's Reign in this world and the next. Those who minister to and for young people must make justice and service an integral part of Catholic youth ministry. As a result, youth ministry will not simply be to and for youth, but will be done with and by them as well.

The Importance of Service Learning

Over the last twenty years, catechetical programs, often those associated with Confirmation preparation for young adolescents, have introduced a service component as a mandatory aspect of the sacramental process. Such additions to catechetical programs seemed to be warranted as the Church continued to reflect on the mission to empower young people to discipleship. Service components, however, were often met with a lack of understanding or in some cases outright hostility. Often it appeared that enthusiastic and well-meaning youth ministers and other catechists created hoops for youth to jump through. It became clear that service activities and projects that were disconnected from an education or catechetical component were limited in their effectiveness and had minimum impact on the young people and on those who were served. Something was missing!

Under the direction of leaders in service-oriented organizations, for example, Catholic Relief Services and the Catholic Campaign for

Human Development, as well as leaders in the field of youth ministry, the development of a service-learning component emerged. Service and ministry on behalf of justice were not to happen in a vacuum or simply because it seemed like a good idea. Such activity needed to be set within the context of the evangelical mission of the Christian community and Catholic social teaching as it is outlined and presented by the bishops of the Church. The bishops spoke of the educational challenge that presented itself to parents, pastors, teachers of religion, catechists, and youth ministers:

> Catholic schools, religious education, adult education and faith formation programs are vitally important for sharing the substance and values of Catholic social teaching. Just as the social teaching of the Church is integral to Catholic faith, the social justice dimensions of teaching are integral to Catholic education and catechesis. . . . Without our social teaching, schools, catechetical programs and other formation programs would be offering an incomplete presentation of our Catholic tradition. (*Sharing Catholic Social Teaching*, pp. 6–7)

With the emergence of service learning and systematic and intentional catechesis around Catholic social teaching, theory and practice could become a comprehensive whole that challenged young people and their family and friends to a commitment to serve as Jesus served.

The Two Feet of Justice: Direct Service and Social Change

In *Poverty and FaithJustice: An Adult Education Program in Christian Discipleship in the United States,* the Catholic Campaign for Human Development provides a framework, or plan of action, for social action. Appendix 1 of that document succinctly outlines a course of action: the work for justice and peace in the world requires two approaches, or prongs, in order to be truly effective and have lasting impact.

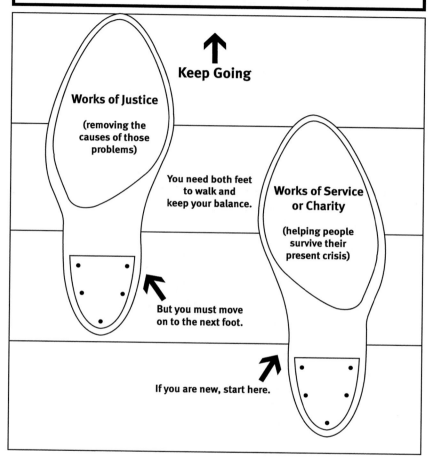

Two Feet of Service and Justice

Keep Going

Works of Justice

(removing the
causes of those
problems)

You need both feet
to walk and
keep your balance.

**Works of Service
or Charity**

(helping people
survive their
present crisis)

But you must move
on to the next foot.

If you are new, start here.

This chart is from *Poverty and FaithJustice: An Adult Education Program on Christian Discipleship in the United States,* by Rev. Ronald C. Chochol (Washington, DC: United States Conference of Catholic Bishops, Inc. [USCCB], 1998), page 20. Copyright © 1998 by the USCCB, Inc.

"We are called as a Church to respond to people's present needs or crises, such as homelessness or hunger" (*Renewing the Vision,* p. 38). In direct service, individuals and groups provide services and resources directly to those who are in need. For example, the person who spends his or her lunch break at the local soup kitchen or the group of young people that make and distribute sandwiches to homeless people provide direct service to others.

In addition is the need to work for social change and to provide advocacy on behalf of individuals and groups that are in need. A key insight is that social problems are often systemic and in some ways institutionalized. "We are also called to help change the policies, structures, and systems that perpetuate injustice through legislative advocacy, community organizing, and work with social change organizations" (*Renewing the Vision,* p. 38). Whether it is the cycle of poverty that plagues many of the families in the inner city and rural areas or the growing number of families and individuals that cannot afford health insurance or the level of violence that permeates every segment of American society or a culture that permits society's most vulnerable to be disposed of, the root causes and ultimate solutions to those problems must be confronted through action that seeks to change societal attitudes and practices.

Effective work for justice necessarily includes both approaches, and the Church in her social teaching calls for its members as well as society at large to take both approaches (to stand on two feet) in the cause of justice. Direct service can be effective only up to a point. Although direct service is an important dimension of social action and, in fact, an indispensable part of the Church's ministry, it goes only so far in providing solutions to poverty, racism, respect for life, oppression, and other social problems. Catholic social teaching has always understood that attempts at social change are also integral elements in the work for justice, peace, and human dignity. Whether it is a letter-writing campaign for legislators to support a medical prescription plan for the elderly or the Right to Life rally that takes place on the Mall in Washington, D.C., every January, the importance of working for social change cannot be underemphasized.

Youth Ministry and Direct Service

For anyone who genuinely cares for young people and enjoys working with them, the opportunity to work side by side on a project or an activity is a rewarding endeavor. Young people have a great desire to make a difference, and they learn best when theory and principle are supported and reinforced with hands-on activities and application. The role of direct service in the work of justice and service can have a tremendous impact on the lives of the young people involved. Direct service brings young people into contact with those who often struggle or are overwhelmed with the cares and concerns of everyday life. Such contact necessarily draws people out of themselves and challenges them to see situations and reality from a different perspective. Young people will often acknowledge, after an opportunity for direct service with someone in need, just how fortunate they are, as they recognize the advantages they have.

Direct service also has the added advantage of gathering young people to work on a common project. Whether it is a clothing or food drive, a day spent playing Bingo with the elderly, or a work-camp experience, it is something that is done with other teens and adults and provides an opportunity for community building and shared experience.

Finally, when young people are involved in direct service, they provide an example to the rest of the faith community about the importance of service to others. It is imperative that youth ministry leaders, catechists and teachers, and service-project coordinators draw attention to what the youth of the parish or school are doing so that parents, faculty, and parishioners understand the effect of such service. The example of teens working for justice also serves as a powerful reminder that the adult community should also be about the work of justice. Caring adults should serve not only as mentors and guides but also as partners who actively pursue service and social action as a part of their own Christian vocation.

Youth Ministry and Social Change

Although young people are readily drawn into direct service on behalf of those in need, it is somewhat more difficult to involve them in the work for social change. Direct-service programs have the advantage of producing results immediately. A person is hungry, so give him or her a sandwich. An immigrant family needs clothing and household supplies, so organize a collection. But achieving social change with results that are long term or systemic is another matter altogether. Young people naturally want to do something that makes a difference and has an immediate impact. Most adults do as well. Effecting long-lasting change, however, can be a lengthy process and involve actions and programs that may seem ineffective. (The American civil rights movement and equality for people of color is a prime example.) Unfortunately, many ministry leaders shy away from social action because attempts to change unjust social structures can be met with resistance when community members hold varying stances and positions regarding social issues, public policies, and activism. As a result of that reality, the temptation is to involve young people in direct service only and to leave social action to the adults in an attempt to avoid controversy. Yet it is vital for youth that high school campus ministers, parishes, and schools educate them on the necessity of working for social change. Through seminars, simulation activities, and reflection, young people can be presented with the larger picture and challenged not to be satisfied with a "one foot" approach to service. Immersion experiences that gather teens to experience the life of poor or disenfranchised people have also been effective when coupled with education and reflection opportunities.

Parish and school service-learning programs also provide opportunities to present the importance of social action in the ministry of justice and service. At Confirmation programs, in religious education sessions, and on retreats, outside speakers as well as role-plays, discussions, and problem-solving activities can prove effective. An activity or discussion that effectively presents a decision for the young people to make engages them while it forces them to see the larger picture.

Providing a variety of social-action opportunities makes it possible to involve young people with varying interests. Lobbying at the state capitol may appeal to some, while tutoring an inner-city child may work for others. Whatever the venue, ministry leaders should use it as an opportunity to meet young people where they are and then bring them to the next level of involvement. For example, tutoring in an inner-city school could lead the tutor to become angry about the lack of resources that exist in most urban school systems. The opportunity then exists to engage that young person in advocacy for improved public education, as long as a clear set of issues is articulated, with an advocacy agenda to go along with it. In their desire to make a difference in the world, young people's vision and understanding can be expanded. Effective youth ministry calls the young Church to strive for justice through service that is both direct and looks to bring about change and reform:

> The ministry of justice and service *nurtures* in young people a social consciousness and a commitment to a life of justice and service rooted in their faith in Jesus Christ, in the Scriptures, and in Catholic social teaching; *empowers* young people to work for justice by concrete efforts to address the causes of human suffering; and *infuses* the concepts of justice, peace, and human dignity into all ministry efforts. (*Renewing the Vision*, p. 38)

Establishing a Service Component for Youth Ministry

The foundational principle for calling young people to service is directly related to the second goal for youth ministry from *Renewing the Vision*, "to draw young people to responsible participation in the life, mission, and work of the Catholic faith community" (p. 11). Frequently there is an attitude among the adult Church that associates young people with the Church of the future. It has become evident, however, especially with the pontificate of John Paul II, that young people are to be seen as a dynamic and integral part of the Church now, and not simply for the future. Furthermore, youth ministry programs should not create service projects that are separate and distinct from those already in existence at the parish or school. At least not entirely! That is particularly true for parish youth ministry. It is important to invite the youth of the parish to become participants in the work of the Catholic faith community as it already exists.

Strategies
for Establishing Service Programs for Youth

- Partner with parish staff or school administration in creating service projects. Involve parents from the outset.
- Utilize diocesan and community programs and resources. Do not "re-invent the wheel"!
- Call young people to leadership and involve them in planning and preparation for service and justice programming.
- Begin with direct service and gradually introduce social-change projects and strategies.
- Inform the rest of the community about what is taking place. Invite young people to offer witness as to how their service has affected them.
- Be inclusive so that virtually anyone can be included in any ministry.
- Include time for debriefing and reflection. (Remember that young people [especially younger adolescents] are primarily experiential learners. Often cognitive learning follows experience.)
- Always include prayer—before, during, and after.
- Always evaluate, and never be afraid to "go back to the drawing board."
- Show gratitude to all volunteers and participants. Effective praise is invaluable.

Ideas for Direct Service and Social Change

The following list, though not exhaustive, offers some wonderful opportunities for service and work for justice that appeal to young people:

- Work camps and home repair ministries—for example, Habitat for Humanity and the Appalachian Service Project—offer quality interaction between adults and youth and present challenges quite different from those young people encounter in their "normal" environment.
- Soup kitchen service and sandwich-making opportunities exist in virtually every city and town in America. Age restrictions at soup kitchens can sometimes prevent middle school teens from participating, but sandwich making can include all ages.

- Outreach to elderly people and shut-ins can often be overlooked in many parishes and schools, but the presence of young people is a welcome respite from the humdrum of daily life for many elderly people. Weekly Bible vigils, Bingo games, Valentine's Day dances, and "adopt a grandparent" events led by the youth are excellent activities that are easy to organize. Visits to facilities that care for senile patients and Alzheimer's patients, though trying at times, can make an extraordinary difference for those individuals.
- Petition drives are often good starters for involving young people in ministry that focuses on social change. Asking young people to staff a table with petitions concerning capital punishment, the right to life, or care for the environment can open their eyes to larger concerns.
- Participation at lobby nights of local and state politicians is an activity that increases awareness of the Catholic legislative agenda and the workings of the political system.
- Programs like Catholic Relief Services' Operation Rice Bowl during Lent can serve a dual purpose. Through regular monetary contributions and a detailed educational program that is easily incorporated into regular catechesis, young people can perform direct service and grow in awareness of world hunger and poverty.
- Support and outreach to troubled youth is another way young people can do direct service and act as advocates for those in need. Programs arranged at local high schools or parishes can be developed with regular visits through the year. The support and friendship of another teen can have a huge influence on the life of a young person who feels abandoned and unloved.

Conclusion

The component of justice and service must be an integral dimension of authentic, Gospel-based youth ministry. A desire to be for others must lie at the heart of our following Jesus Christ. It is imperative that the young Church be invited to take up the mission of the Church to proclaim and help build the Reign of God in our world. Without the energy, vision, and enthusiasm of the young, the Church's ministry will never be complete and Christ's call to recognize him in the "least of these" will cease to confront the conscience of those who would live only for themselves.

Chapter Questions

1. Cite some examples from Jesus's ministry that illustrate his outreach and concern for the poor and oppressed.
2. In Matthew 25:31–46 Jesus clearly associates God's final judgment with recognizing God's presence in the poor, the needy, and the oppressed. Do you think the work of justice is more important than the quest for personal holiness? Why or why not? How could they be connected?
3. How would you respond to someone who says that Catholic social teaching promotes the liberal agenda? the conservative agenda?
4. How would you proceed in catechizing the parish or school community on the need for service activities for youth?
5. Why do you think mandatory service activities should or should not be part of sacramental preparation (particularly Confirmation) for young people?
6. Propose some concrete strategies for taking young people from a "one foot" to a "two feet" approach to social action.

Chapter 10

Youth Ministry:
The Component of Leadership Development

Greg "Dobie" Moser

Introduction

One of the strengths of Catholic youth ministry acknowledged by other denominations is the emphasis on enabling young people for leadership. That emphasis has taken on a new urgency in our Church and in our society. In a culture of violence, racism, individualism, and materialism, we are faced with forming the next generation of leaders. If young people are to take their rightful role in society and in the Church, they must be provided with the necessary skills, relationships, and vision.

Objectives

This chapter explores the importance of youth as leaders in youth ministry and beyond, identifies the key leadership principles and qualities in youth ministry, identifies the needs of youth leaders, and presents structures for leadership development programming.

The Ministry of Youth Leadership Development

"True ministry duplicates itself."

This quote from the United States Catholic Conference's *Vision of Youth Ministry* (p. 10) continues to have relevance for ministry with young people. When adult leaders in youth ministry invest time and energy in the training and formation of young people, the results are amazing. Young people become empowered to provide leadership for their peers in youth ministry groups, with adults in parish ministries, and among their friends and fellow students at school and in the community. They grow in confidence, have the skills necessary to participate fully in the life of the parish, and develop the abilities necessary to be a strong witness of faith. This investment in the young people of the parish has a long-term impact on the young people and on our Church and society.

As *Renewing the Vision* states: "We strongly encourage all ministry leaders and communities to call forth the gifts of all young people and empower them for ministry to their peers and leadership in our faith communities. We need their gifts, energy, and vitality" (p. 42).

Why Youth Leadership?

Leadership is the ministry of all baptized persons. As a baptized Christian, every person has a responsibility to determine what role God is asking her or him to take in the Church and in the world. Leadership is one response to that call, and needs to be valued and cultivated as a way to develop and use one's gifts.

Ministry leaders need to value young people for their role now, while preparing them to serve well in the future. Many of today's adult youth ministry leaders benefited from loving and supportive adults who believed in them as leaders when they were young. The Church's ministry with adolescents seeks to "cultivate the gifts and talents of young people, and empower them to utilize these gifts and talents in leadership and ministry in the Church and community including peer ministry and intergenerational skills" (*Renewing the Vision*, pp. 17–18).

Young people have countless gifts to discover, share, and develop in service to the Church and to the world. Our Church is in great need of their gifts. Without their gifts and presence, the Church is incomplete and unable to fully live as a Christian community.

When youth are valued as leaders, they know they belong and are needed to carry on the mission of the Church and the Gospel. The second goal in *Renewing the Vision* calls the Church as a whole "to draw young people to responsible participation in the life, mission, and work of the . . . faith community" (p. 11).

Leadership in the Church and Beyond

The call to leadership must be understood in two basic arenas: the Church and society. In the Church, leadership is an important expression of ministry. In drawing young people into responsible participation, ministry leaders are challenged to involve youth in the liturgical, pastoral, and social outreach life of the faith community. That prepares young people for a role in a participative Church. But they must also be enabled to deal with the realities of parish life: for example, who controls the keys? the rooms? the budget? That is an important arena in which to involve young people. Simultaneously, young people must be prepared for participation and leadership in the larger society. In that arena, leadership might be understood as discipleship. Young people are called to the ministry of the marketplace, those places where they live, play, work, and go to school. They will be, and they are already, leaders in many of those areas. How can this leadership become discipleship? Young people want spirituality and a Gospel challenge that fits all areas of their lives: their relationships, their family, their neighborhood, and the streets. How can they bring their Christian values to their reality? How can young people transform and evangelize their culture? The challenge is to prepare young people for leadership in both arenas.

Operational Principles of Youth Leadership

Principle 1: Rooted in Ministerial Relationships

Young people experience Gospel love through relationships with caring, committed adults. Ministry is rooted in such relationships. Adults who love God and are active members of the faith community, who love young people and value them as being made in God's image and likeness will accept young people where they are while calling them to become more on behalf of the Gospel.

Principle 2: Integrate Faith and Prayer

Young people have a deep hunger for holiness, even when they have not articulated or integrated that hunger into their identity. Leadership is as much about building a loving Christian environment rooted in faith as it is about achieving great program results. Integrating Catholic spirituality, theology, and teaching into leadership formation is vital in order to pass on Gospel values that serve as a foundation for Christian leadership.

Yet many youth do not see themselves as leaders, or they may have a narrow or ill-defined understanding of leadership. Actively seeking out youth and inviting them into leadership by making connections with what is happening in their lives is vital. Seeking out the quiet faithful who may not recognize their giftedness, as well as those who have begun to answer the call to leadership, is equally important.

Principle 3: Respect, Support, and Encourage Other Activities

Using time effectively is a top priority as teens (and adults) balance many competing demands in their busy lives. Letting them know the different levels of involvement required of leadership in a timely manner enables them to make informed decisions that teach responsibility and commitment.

Principal 4: Build Meaningful Roles

Young people need to experience a genuine partnership with adults regarding decision making, how power is exercised, and how people are treated. Teens can help identify needs; determine priorities and set goals; plan, implement, and evaluate programs; and much more. A common error is to underestimate the capabilities of young leaders and therefore lose them through boredom or the lack of a challenge to do meaningful work. Youth ministers need to seek a time balance regarding relationships, tasks, and formation for leaders. That enables young people to reinforce their role in the Christian community, to learn the demands of leadership and their role in responding, and to be continually shaped as the servant leaders described in John's Gospel:

> "You call me Teacher and Lord—and you are right, for that is what I am. So if I, your Lord and Teacher, have washed your feet, you also ought to wash one another's feet. For I have set you an example, that you also should do as I have done to you." (13:13–15)

Principle 5:
Build on Existing Strengths and Assets

There are people in every institution who have a deep love of young people and express it in ways that make the world better for teens and families. Consider the work of the Search Institute, which has identified forty assets that help an entire community support young people on their path to healthy adulthood. The external assets include support, empowerment, boundaries and expectations, and the constructive use of time. The internal assets include a commitment to learning, positive values, social competencies, and a positive identity.

What Youth Leaders Need

Young people need loving relationships with adults who believe in them. They need to be in an environment that is emotionally, psychologically, and physically safe. They need to know that adults expect the best of them and believe in them and will provide them with the space to grow and risk. They need to know that adults value them as equals while recognizing the differences in their roles and relationship.

Youth leaders need to have the opportunity to deal with the natural consequences of their decisions and actions. An eighth-grade camper described it this way on his evaluation of a week at CYO camp: "We need to learn to sit at the feet of our own experience. Everything that happens to you is your teacher. It is either a lesson that is also a blessing, or a blessing that is also a lesson" (anonymous).

Young people also need healthy and supportive relationships with their peers. That includes the opportunity to get to know one another while discovering their own gifts and limitations and those of others. Young leaders need to know that their peers depend on them and are capable of giving to one another, especially on behalf of a common goal.

Leaders of all ages need to recognize that they can always learn and discover more about themselves, others, and the challenge of leadership. Every leadership meeting affords an opportunity to learn new information or a new way of doing things. Leadership, like the life of faithful discipleship, always calls us to become more on behalf of the Gospel.

Developing Leadership Training

These five basic characteristics for leadership must be integrated into leadership development programs for young people:

- *A guiding vision.* A leader must have a clear sense of what he or she wants to do and the strength to persist in the face of setbacks. It begins with an overall goal for youth leadership development and specific objectives for particular training experiences. In ministry, the Reign of God is that guiding vision!
- *Passion.* A leader must love what she or he does. Young people have a natural passion. The challenge is to awaken that passion and foster a sense of excitement by enabling young people to see that they are building the Reign of God.
- *Integrity.* A leader possesses self-knowledge, candor, and maturity. Leadership development training must challenge young people to mesh their actions with their values. Enabling young people to assess how well their faith values are integrated into their family, school, and neighborhood lives is vital.
- *Trust.* In leadership, trust is earned and given. When calling young people into leadership roles, ministry leaders extend trust. As young people develop the skills and characteristics of Christian leaders, they are able to earn further trust.
- *Curiosity and daring.* A leader wonders about everything and is willing to take risks. Leadership development should foster that critical thinking and curiosity and must not squash it with too much structure and bureaucracy.

Training must include practical skills for planning, problem solving, decision making, goal setting, and facilitating meetings. Additionally, young people need to be provided with training in skills that are necessary for effective leadership: active listening, conflict management, community building, motivating others, and time and stress management.

Young people also need to have opportunities to slow down and listen to the thoughts and feelings going on inside them. They need to grapple with questions of meaning while trying to determine what God is asking of them. Teens need to learn how to sort out the different perspectives and voices in their lives while attempting to assign meanings to their experiences in an integrated manner. Leadership training must enable young people to build confidence and self-worth, help them clarify their values and beliefs, and develop a sense of community and support.

It is also important to foster critical thinking and reflecting skills. Young people need to be empowered to ask the right questions and to ask the hard questions (the "why" and "why not" questions about involvement in Church, justice in society, and so forth).

Leadership skills and formation require that young people deal with the specific realities of their local setting. Yet leadership in a Christian context requires movement toward a coherent worldview that sees all persons as our brothers and sisters in Christ. Young leaders therefore need not be sheltered from difficult and vexing issues in the Church and in society. The Gospel belief in the dignity of all persons as made in the image and likeness of God challenges Christians to see others as our brothers and sisters in Christ. It is a call to action on behalf of justice in our family, in our community, and far beyond.

Calling Forth Youth Leaders

Preparing youth for leadership is a process. It is raising young people's consciousness that leadership is not only possible but desirable and part of being Christian. It is a genuine movement toward discipleship. Some practical steps include these:

- *Surface their gifts and call young people forth individually.* Affirming each person's giftedness is the first step. Young people need to know that the gift of leadership is seen within each of them. It is up to ministry leaders to call forth those gifts for the community.
- *Equip them with the skills for leadership.* It is essential to provide the practical skills necessary for the roles to which young people are called.
- *Connect youth with opportunities to serve and lead.* The role of the ministry leader is to enable youth to use their gifts. Start with trial runs where they can practice their skills in smaller groups and

relaxed situations. Even Jesus sent the disciples out two by two to minister, and then had them come back and compare their experiences and learnings.

- *Provide support for young people.* They must be provided with support and encouragement. Adults need to serve as mentors, modeling for young people what service, leadership, and ministry mean in the community.
- *Provide a vision!* This is critical. Young people are called to be partners in the tradition of the faith community. They are called to build the Reign of God, and that is a noble adventure! A shared vision provides the reason and purpose behind the call to leadership.

The Payoffs

What are the benefits of involving young people in leadership?
- Throughout their lives young people will bring vitality, creativity, and generosity of time and energy to others, including their family, their school environment, their faith community, and society at large.
- Throughout their lives they will be more sensitive and empathetic to others.
- They will take on a more active role in the Church, perhaps even choosing a career in ministry as a volunteer or a professional.
- They will take on a more active role in society, building the Reign of God in the "marketplace."
- They will enhance their own search for God and form a deeper spirituality.
- They will like themselves more, and feel good about themselves because they are doing good work. They will be happier.
- They will push, pull, lead, and drag the Church into a more inclusive, participative, and hopeful future.

The Role of the Adult

Ministry leaders can provide several things when calling young people to leadership:

- *Permission.* Adult leaders need to take the first step in inviting young people into leadership, taking them seriously and moving beyond token responsibility. Young people must be enabled to make decisions, take ownership, and become invested.
- *Protection.* Adult leaders need to protect young people from chaos by orienting and training them in their leadership roles. Assisting them in setting realistic goals and providing clear descriptions of their roles is crucial. Young people should be given responsibility appropriate for their skill and maturity level. That requires a sensitive and trusting relationship between young people and youth ministers.
- *Support.* Adult leaders need to affirm the gifts and talents of young people. Providing necessary training and giving honest feedback and evaluation on contributions, strengths, and weaknesses in their roles is also necessary. Young people must be enabled to deal with societal, Church, educational, and employment structures and systems that are often overwhelming and frustrating for them. Adult leaders can help them deal with the frustrations of working within those structures and hierarchies.
- *Empowerment.* Adult leaders need to connect young people with opportunities for leadership in parish youth programs, in other areas of parish life (inviting young people onto parish committees), and in secular arenas. It is also the role of ministry leaders to encourage and support youth's ownership in those areas. Empowerment is a process of creating involvement and ownership.
- *Mentoring.* Adult leaders must model what it means to be mature Christian believers and what it means to be a leader in the Church and in society. All of us are called to be disciples—people who challenge young people to witness of the Gospel in all areas of their lives; and enablers—people who empower young people to become responsible participants in leadership. Mentors walk with young people on their journey in faith and through leadership.

Conclusion

Our Church and the world face significant challenges. We have a wonderful opportunity to grow leadership together. We have the chance to serve youth in the Church while equipping them with what they need to change the world into the image and likeness of God. Training and mentoring young people into leadership enriches the Church now and also plants seeds for the future. It enables young people to live their faith and leadership roles in every facet of society. By inviting youth into Christian leadership, we send an implicit message that we believe in young people, have high expectations for their present and future abilities, and expect them to handle difficult challenges. Such a nurturing and supportive environment enables youth and adults to grow in discipleship. Our Church and the world need the life and vitality of our young people, and they deserve the opportunity to do their part. If we neglect them and deny them leadership opportunities, we do so at our present and future peril.

Chapter Questions

1. What opportunities exist for young people to exercise leadership in your faith community?
2. Identify the parish, school, community, and diocesan training programs for young people and adults that develop leadership skills and qualities.
3. How broad is the role of youth leadership in your thoughts about parish life?
4. How are you open to the various ways youth make a difference for the good of others?
5. What aspects of your parish's life could be more infused with young people?
6. What gifts do young people bring to leadership roles in your parish?

Chapter 11

Youth Ministry: The Component of Pastoral Care

Robert J. McCarty, DMin

Introduction

The 1997 document *Renewing the Vision* states that the third goal for youth ministry is "to foster the total personal and spiritual growth of each young person" (p. 15). Youth ministry, therefore, is intentional in addressing the unique developmental and spiritual needs of youth and in nurturing the qualities or assets essential for holistic adolescent development. Further, we are reminded that comprehensive youth ministry also assists youth in addressing personal and societal obstacles to healthy growth. The ministry of pastoral care is the component in comprehensive youth ministry that promotes healthy adolescent development, addresses crisis issues, and supports the families of young people.

Objectives

This chapter explores the principles and methods for caring for young people and their families, provides a framework for fostering positive adolescent development, outlines a comprehensive approach to the pastoral care of adolescents, and provides a nonprofessional approach to crisis intervention.

The Definition of Pastoral Care

In youth ministry the component of pastoral care is an invitation to return to pastoring, to that ongoing process of caring deeply for young people, confronting them honestly when necessary, meeting young people where they are, and showing them the rich possibilities of human wholeness. Pastoral care is an invitation to conversion in a holistic sense.

Pastoral care is also a ministry of compassionate and intrusive presence. We are challenged to surround young people with the best possible adult support systems; to connect young people with a web of family, youth ministers, teachers, and significant adults;

and to be a compassionate presence in their lives. And our presence is intrusive when necessary. We challenge and confront negative or harmful behaviors, values, and attitudes, and we witness to Gospel values and lifestyles.

Understanding Positive Adolescent Development

Pastoral care is essentially about fostering positive adolescent development, the process through which young people actively seek to meet their basic needs and build their individual assets or competencies, and are assisted in doing so. New research has provided valuable insight into the factors that contribute to healthy adolescent development. The leader in this field has been the Search Institute, whose extensive research has identified forty essential building blocks, or assets, that contribute to positive growth in children and youth.

Search Institute divides the assets into external and internal categories. The external assets are those networks, experiences, relationships, and activities that provide a scaffold or support system for young people through their families, community, school, church, and other organizations. External assets involve key areas of support, empowerment, boundaries and expectations, and use of time. Internal assets are those qualities, life skills, and characteristics that develop within adolescents and relate to their educational commitment, positive values, social competencies, and positive identity. The accompanying chart describes the forty assets.

External Assets

Support

• Family support: Family life provides high levels of love and support.

- Positive family communication: Young person and her or his parent(s) communicate positively, and young person is willing to seek advice and counsel from parent(s).
- Other adult relationships: Young person receives support from three or more nonparent adults.
- Caring neighborhood: Young person experiences caring neighbors.
- Caring school climate: School provides a caring, encouraging environment.
- Parent involvement in schooling: Parent(s) are actively involved in helping young person succeed in school.

Empowerment

- Community values youth: Young person perceives that adults in the community value youth.
- Youth as resources: Young people are given useful roles in the community.
- Service to others: Young person serves in the community one hour or more per week.
- Safety: Young person feels safe at home, at school, and in the neighborhood.

Boundaries and Expectations

- Family boundaries: Family has clear rules and consequences, and monitors the young person's whereabouts.
- School boundaries: School provides clear rules and consequences.
- Neighborhood boundaries: Neighbors take responsibility for monitoring young people's behavior.
- Adult role models: Parent(s) and other adults model positive, responsible behavior.
- Positive peer influence: Young person's best friends model responsible behavior.
- High expectations: Both parent(s) and teachers encourage the young person to do well.

Constructive Use of Time

- Creative activities: Young person spends three or more hours per week in lessons or practice in music, theater, or other arts.
- Youth programs: Young person spends three or more hours per week in sports, clubs, or organizations at school and/or in community organizations.
- Religious community: Young person spends one hour or more per week in activities in a religious institution.
- Time at home: Young person is out with friends "with nothing special to do" two or fewer nights per week.

Internal Assets

Commitment to Learning

- Achievement motivation: Young person is motivated to do well in school.
- School engagement: Young person is actively engaged in learning.
- Homework: Young person reports doing at least one hour of homework every school day.
- Bonding to school: Young person cares about her or his school.
- Reading for pleasure: Young person reads for pleasure three or more hours per week.

Positive Values

- Caring: Young person places high value on helping other people.
- Equality and social justice: Young person places high value on promoting equality and reducing hunger and poverty.
- Integrity: Young person acts on convictions and stands up for her or his beliefs.
- Honesty: Young person "tells the truth even when it is not easy."
- Responsibility: Young person accepts and takes personal responsibility.
- Restraint: Young person believes it is important not to be sexually active or to use alcohol or other drugs.

Social Competencies

- Planning and decision making: Young person knows how to plan ahead and make choices.
- Interpersonal competence: Young person has empathy, sensitivity, and friendship skills.
- Cultural competence: Young person has knowledge of and comfort with people of different cultural/racial/ethnic backgrounds.
- Resistance skills: Young person can resist negative peer pressure and dangerous situations.
- Peaceful conflict resolution: Young person seeks to resolve conflict nonviolently.

Positive Identity

- Personal power: Young person feels he or she has control over "things that happen to me."
- Self-esteem: Young person reports having a high self-esteem.
- Sense of purpose: Young person reports that "my life has a purpose."
- Positive view of personal future: Young person is optimistic about her or his personal future.

The assets identified by Search Institute serve two important functions: they promote positive, healthy behaviors and they protect young people from negative, or risk, behaviors. The more assets present in young people's lives, the more likely they are to be involved in healthy activities, relationships, and experiences.

The asset language and approach dovetails with comprehensive youth ministry and fits especially well with the component of pastoral care. Asset building depends on positive relationships between young people and caring adults, a supportive community that welcomes the involvement of young people, the significant impact and role of the family, and opportunities for young people to use their gifts and develop their life skills. Those experiences are integral to youth ministry. Further, both the individual minister and the general faith community play significant roles in fostering the development of assets and the healthy personal and spiritual growth in youth, reflective of our vision of comprehensive youth ministry.

Principles of Pastoral Care

The following five principles shape the ministry of pastoral care within comprehensive youth ministry.

Pastoral Care Is Not Counseling

Pastoral care is much broader than counseling. All adults are called to be pastoral caregivers, but counseling requires special training and credentials. As caregivers we provide young people with support, guidance, compassionate care, accurate information, and confrontation when necessary. We need to understand adolescent development, the importance of fostering internal and external assets in youth, the impact of family dynamics, and the role of the larger community in supporting young people.

However, in some situations counseling is an expression of pastoral care. When young people's needs require more professional care, pastoral care includes identifying local resources and connecting young people with competent mental-health professionals.

Pastoral Care Is Not Limited to Crisis Situations

Pastoral care is much broader than situational crises; it is an ongoing relationship with individual adolescents and with young people as a group. Pastoral care provides an ongoing pastoral presence integrated throughout a comprehensive youth ministry that is proactive in fostering healthy and holistic adolescent growth.

Pastoral Care
Is a Community Responsibility

Just as ministry with young people is more effective when the entire community understands its role, pastoral care requires a broader ownership than just individual ministers. We are challenged not only to mobilize the local faith community on behalf of young people but also to move beyond the parish and school communities to network with the larger societal community.

Pastoral care requires collaboration with social services, community resources, and educational and governmental organizations to share resources, personnel, and services in order to confront the societal issues of poverty, discrimination, drug abuse, and personal and domestic violence. Effective pastoral care of young people does indeed "take an entire village," and it is the role of the Church to mobilize the village on behalf of young people.

Pastoral Care
Provides Young People with Life Skills

Skills refer to abilities, behaviors, and actions. Many young people lack the life skills necessary for participating in a complex society. Interpersonal skills enable young people to develop relationships, communicate effectively, participate in the world of work and employment, and handle conflict. Examples of intrapersonal skills include decision making, discernment and problem solving, critical reflection, and coping abilities such as time and stress management. Young people also need systemic skills, those abilities that enable them to navigate life in a community of complicated social, educational, employment, and health systems and services.

Pastoral Care
Addresses the Needs of Families

Effective pastoral care responds to young people in their primary context—their family. The changes in family structures and configurations have been significant in the past two generations, affecting young people and parents alike. Moreover, parents often find themselves overwhelmed by the rate of change in society, generally, and in youth culture, specifically.

Pastoral care of adolescents includes strategies and approaches that address families in their entirety, parents in their roles specifically, and young people within this fundamental context. Partnering with parents and providing services to them will strengthen our families and provide effective pastoral care for young people.

Elements of Pastoral Care

The following interdependent elements provide a framework for pastoral care planning.

Promotion Strategies

These are activities, programs, relationships, and experiences that enhance and foster self-esteem and healthy adolescent development. Examples include strategies that teach life skills, foster assets in young people, connect young people with healthy adults, support family activities, educate parish and school staffs, provide parent education, and strategies for youth ministry programming such as retreats, service opportunities, leadership roles, prayer experiences, and community-building activities.

Prevention Strategies

Though closely related to and overlapping with the promotion element, for planning purposes it is useful to consider prevention separately. Prevention strategies include activities, programs, and relationships that prepare young people to confront situations that might engender risk behaviors. Examples include providing education and awareness programs on issues such as depression and suicide, drug and alcohol use, conflict and aggression management, dealing with grief and loss, domestic and relational violence, making sexual decisions, and understanding eating disorders. Prevention strategies also include teaching peer responding skills and resistance and refusal skills.

Crisis Intervention Strategies

These are activities, programs, and relationships that support and respond to young people and families in crisis. Examples include developing a crisis response plan appropriate for groups experiencing crisis, such as responding to young people when a peer dies suddenly or when a suicide has occurred or in times of local and national disasters, such as the shootings at Columbine High School in 1999 and the terrorist attack on the World Trade Center in 2001. This element also includes developing a response for individuals who need personal care or for families that need assistance in dealing with serious issues. Knowing how to access community resources, develop and publicize a resource list, and investigate referral processes are key tasks in crisis intervention.

Advocacy Strategies

This is the systemic dimension of pastoral care. Advocacy refers to the activities, programs, and relationships that work and speak on behalf of young people and their families. Examples include addressing parish, school, and community leadership concerning the needs of adolescents and their families; championing the involvement of young people in parish, school, and community activities; surveying available services and resources and promoting their expansion if inadequate; and mobilizing all sectors of the community on behalf of effective juvenile justice and adolescent health-care processes and facilities.

Crisis Intervention

Though pastoral care is much broader than dealing with crises, responding to young people who are experiencing distress or engaging in risk behaviors is certainly an important aspect of pastoral care. It is essential to remember, however, the difference between counseling and responding. Counseling requires a specific set of skills, training, and expertise. Most all those who minister with youth are not trained as counselors.

However, most adults working with young people can still be effective in responding to young people in crisis by developing the recognition, response, and referral skills needed to provide a caring response to young people when necessary. Recognition skills simply refer to one's ability to see the behavioral signs of an individual or group that is in crisis. Response skills refer to actually reaching out to and making contact with an individual or group that is in crisis, and referral skills include acknowledging that an issue requires a more professional response and identifying potential resources. Adults can indeed be pastoral responders and caregivers.

Anatomy of a Crisis

Whether it may be a life crisis or a crisis brought on by and exhibited in risk behaviors, there is a general pattern to crises that assists the caregiver in responding.

The first stage in a crisis is disruption in a critical area in the life of a young person, such as in family, school, or peer relationships. Disruptions include family issues of divorce, separation, long-term unemployment, death, illness, abuse, frequent moving, and alcohol or drug abuse. School disruptions include feeling pressure to get good grades, receiving failing grades, starting a new school, or failing at a team or club. Disruptions in peer relationships might include the inability to make or keep friends, feeling like an outsider, a lack of physical development, or confusion over sexual identity.

Such disruptions lead to strong feelings in a young person, the second stage in a crisis. Depending on the disruption, the young person might experience a broad range of emotions: anger, loneliness, depression, apathy, guilt, fear, feeling trapped, sadness, or confusion. The key in this stage is that anything one feels strongly on the inside has to come out somehow. That is the third stage.

If a young person does not have the opportunity to verbalize and ventilate feelings to a trusted person, then oftentimes the feelings are expressed in behaviors. Such behaviors might include sullen or secluded times at home, sudden outbursts of anger or intense emotion, or more serious behaviors, including running away, cutting oneself, developing eating disorders, engaging in delinquent acts, using drugs or alcohol, being sexually promiscuous, or committing suicide.

Often the crises that occur in the lives of young people are a natural though painful part of life. The breakdown of significant relationships, family issues, school problems, confusion over the future, and the death of a family member or friend are experiences shared generally by everyone. Sometimes the crisis affects an entire group of young people, as in the death of a peer. In such cases the response will include communal elements, such as group prayer, small-group sharing processes, attending a funeral or viewing together, creating memorials, or participating in similar activities.

However, the following set of "risk" behaviors are more harmful and dangerous, and need specific description.

Youth at Risk

For this chapter, youth at risk are those who by circumstances or choice are in situations that expose them to failure or harm in their personal, social, familial, or spiritual lives. Some young people live in situations beyond their control that contribute to the possibility of risk behaviors. Other young people choose to engage in behaviors or situations that might cause them harm.

The inability to meet basic physical, relational, emotional, and psychological needs; poor coping skills; and inadequate support systems contribute to a teen's vulnerability for harmful behaviors. Research has found common antecedents or circumstances, which, though not direct causes of risk behaviors, do identify circumstances that lead to a greater possibility of such behaviors. These antecedents of risk behaviors can themselves have a negative impact on young people:

- Doing poorly in school, or expecting to do poorly, predicts all problem behaviors.
- Early initiation of any risk behavior predicts heavier involvement in that behavior later.
- Impulsive behavior, truancy, and antisocial behaviors are related to all other risk behaviors.
- Low resistance to peer influences and having friends who are engaged in risk behaviors impacts a young person's ability to make good choices about behaviors.
- Insufficient bonding to parents, inadequate supervision and communication with parents, and parents who are too authoritative or too permissive impacts behavior.

- Living in a poverty area or high-density urban area can be a difficult circumstance for young people.
- Rare church attendance contributes to risk behavior.

Adults who build trusting relationships with young people can develop recognition skills to see the disruptions, name the emotions, and assist young people in finding healthier ways to express their feelings. This does not replace counseling; it is a nonprofessional approach to crisis intervention that utilizes problem-solving techniques.

A Crisis Intervention Approach

A nonprofessional pastoral response to young people is guided by the following principles:
- Caregivers need to listen twice as much as they talk when assisting teens in crisis. The most essential skill for caregiving is genuine listening.
- Caregivers need to guide the decision-making process. The pastoral responder must resist the temptation to solve young people's problems, to rescue them from their pains, or to become a font of advice.
- Caregivers need to be advocates for young people who are hurting. The pastoral responder can accompany young people in crisis as they navigate family, societal, social, or educational systems. Those ministering with youth can enable young people to find their voice, if necessary, and facilitate situations where that voice can be heard.
- Caregivers need to express and receive honest emotions. The pastoral responder allows individuals or a group of young people to vent and ventilate the feelings that may have been bottled up inside by listening in a nonjudgmental manner and asking clarifying questions to assist them in accurately naming their emotions.
- Caregivers need to extend realistic hope in the midst of crisis. The pastoral responder enables young people in crisis to gain perspective in a situation that may seem overwhelming and confusing. By assisting young people in naming their problems, identifying possible solutions, discovering possible resources and supports, and expressing their feelings, caregivers bring hope. That hope, however, must be realistic. Sometimes relationships are not

healthy, families do not work out their differences, or expectations are not realized. Sometimes the best that happens is problem management, not resolution.

The following is a five-step process for the approach to crisis intervention. That approach, though described for responding to an individual, can easily be adapted to a group setting.

Make Contact

The first step includes either the young person coming to the adult and asking for advice or assistance or the adult going to the young person, or group of young people, because the adult perceives an issue. When the adult has to make the initial contact, it is important that she or he identify the observable behaviors that have caused concern: "I saw you doing . . ." or "I was there when you . . ." or "You seem to be feeling ___ because you said ___." Anchor your concern in observable behavior.

Gather Information

Let the young person tell his or her story if it's an individual crisis, or elicit information from the group if it's a shared experience, such as the death of a classmate or parish member. Ask good clarifying questions and utilize effective reflective-listening skills. That is an essential step in "naming" the problem accurately.

Explore Solutions

In this step the individual or group is encouraged to brainstorm the possible responses to the issue and to identify potential consequences. The caregiver's role is to facilitate the individual's or group's problem solving, rather than provide advice. By enabling the young person or people to identify a response, ownership is created for the solution because it is their solution, not the responder's.

Develop a Plan

Assist the young person or people in identifying the concrete steps that might be taken. Those steps should be simple, specific, doable, and short-term actions that include who will do what, when, where, and how. Regardless of whether the issue is a family, school, personal, or relationship issue, practical action steps with a realistic timeline are essential.

For serious issues the plan might involve referral to a professional or a community resource.

Follow Up

The responder should set a time for meeting again to evaluate the action steps. This builds in accountability and assures the young people that the adult responder is committed to providing ongoing support.

Two additional issues need to be considered: confidentiality and referral. It is important that the adult responder define confidentiality prior to any one-on-one conversations and explain the limits of confidentiality. Confidentiality never applies when there is a possibility of a young person hurting herself or himself, hurting another person, or being hurt by someone else. In addition, young people must never be told that they cannot disclose any portion of a conversation (including behaviors) between themselves and an adult.

In many states youth ministers and ministry volunteers are obligated by law to report to the authorities any suspicion that a child or young person is being maltreated. Youth ministry leaders should check with their local diocesan offices and with the local county attorney's office for more complete information about the legal obligation to protect children.

Sometimes the presenting issue or crisis requires outside professional care. A responder who lacks the time needed to walk with the young person through a crisis, the skill to assist a young person, or the emotional security for the specific issue must refer. Emotional security is threatened when an issue strikes a personal chord in the responder. Perhaps the responder experienced abuse or alcoholism in the past and cannot respond honestly to a young person experiencing the same, or perhaps sexual identity, pregnancy, or abortion are issues about which a responder has strong values and cannot respond objectively to a young person. Regardless of the reason, when an issue elicits a strong emotional response, the responder needs to refer.

However, referring to a professional is not a ministry failure. Rather, it is effective pastoral care, especially if the responder explains honestly why the referral is necessary, assists the young person in finding the appropriate resource, and continues to make contact and follow up with the young person.

Chapter Questions

1. What strategies or opportunities exist in your community to foster the development of assets in young people?
2. What intentional approaches exist for developing social, personal, and life skills in young people?
3. What intentional activities and strategies exist to support and strengthen the families of young people?
4. What plan is in place for responding to a crisis affecting the youth community, as well as responding to individuals who are experiencing crisis?
5. What community resources are available to support a response to a young person who is engaging in risk behaviors?

Chapter 12

Youth Ministry:
The Component of Prayer and Worship

Randy Raus with Laurie Delgatto

Introduction

From the Scriptures and Tradition, we come to know prayer as a response to God's invitation of covenant and communion. Prayer involves the whole being—mind, body, and soul. We gather in prayer to petition God for help, to give praise and thanks, to seek reconciliation, and sometimes to mark a special occasion.

By teaching young people to pray, ministry leaders can open for them a way to communicate on a deeply personal level with God, who is the source of all holiness. By inviting them to explore different forms of personal prayer, ministry leaders encourage young people to expand their image of God and their understanding of prayer. By challenging young people to look at communal prayer, ministry leaders remind them of their role in building God's Reign and as a part of the Body of Christ.

Objectives

This chapter provides an overview of the ministry of prayer and worship and identifies practical and intentional ways to draw young people into full, active, and conscious participation in the prayer and liturgical life of the Church.

Nonliturgical Prayer and Young People

The earliest followers of Jesus knew the power of prayer. In a letter to the Ephesians, Paul said, "Pray in the Spirit at all times" (6:18). To the Thessalonians Paul wrote, "Pray without ceasing, give thanks in all circumstances; for this is the will of God in Christ Jesus for you" (1 Thessalonians 5:17–18).

The *Catechism* offers three fundamental facts of faith about prayer:

- *"It is always possible to pray"* (no. 2743).
- *"Prayer is a vital necessity"* (no. 2744).
- "Prayer and *Christian life* are *inseparable"* (no. 2745).

From the early Christians, we come to know that praying is not simply something one does. Rather, it is an orientation to life. However, "in order to pray, one must have the will to pray . . . [and] one must also learn how to pray. Through a living transmission (Sacred Tradition) within 'the believing and praying Church,'[11] the Holy Spirit teaches the children of God how to pray" (*CCC,* no. 2650).

From the Scriptures we come to know prayer as the response to God's invitation of covenant and communion. We express the covenant relationship with God in prayers of blessing and adoration, petition and contrition, intercession, thanksgiving, and praise. Through prayer we respond to God's invitation to communion.

The job of ministry leaders is to help youth enter more deeply into covenantal relationship with God and experience the communion that God has prepared for them in love:

> The ministry of prayer and worship *celebrates* and *deepens* young people's relationship with Jesus Christ through the bestowal of grace, communal prayer, and liturgical experiences; it *awakens* their awareness of the spirit at work in their lives; it *incorporates* young people more fully into the sacramental life of the Church, especially Eucharist; it *nurtures* the personal prayer life of young people; and it *fosters* family rituals and prayers. (*Renewing the Vision*, p. 44)

This paragraph from the United States Conference of Catholic Bishops' document on youth ministry describes the breadth of the ministry of prayer and worship. Some foundational principles are evident in this vision.

Prayer Is About Community

Young people's prayers join them to the heart of our loving God. That relationship is celebrated in community. Youth ministry leaders are called to help youth grow in their personal prayer life, their prayer with their family, their prayer in community, and their full participation with the whole faith community at prayer in the sacraments, especially the central prayer of our faith, the liturgy of the Eucharist. The very act of prayer binds us as a community.

Prayer Is Integrating and Holistic

Prayer and worship is more than putting aside a few minutes for an opening or closing prayer. What the Church strives for in its ministry with young people, then, is not so much a program filled with prayers but a truly prayerful youth ministry.

Prayerful youth ministry is about praying always and praying in all ways. Every part of our lives is a matter worthy of God's time in our personal prayer. In the same way, everything done in youth ministry can be brought to prayer. "Opportunities for prayer in peer, family, and intergenerational settings allow youth to experience the fullness of prayer styles in the church's tradition. . . . For this reason youth leaders and catechists need to provide a variety of traditional and contemporary prayer experiences for and with youth" (*From Age to Age*, no. 58).

The ministry of prayer and worship is not separate from the other components of youth ministry; it is an integral part of ministry with young people. When youth are learning about the faith, ministry leaders must take time to pray that the learning seeds fall on good ground. When they learn about justice and serving those who are in need, young people should pray for an attitude of service and for the strength to change their own lives. When sharing the Good News with others, young people need to pray to stay humble and courageous. When learning about leadership, young people need to pray to be foot-washers and leaders modeled after Jesus. Prayer must be at the center of all youth ministry efforts. It is the unseen but very real power that makes ministry with young people truly forceful and life changing.

Praying with Youth

To help youth participate actively in the parish community, youth ministry leaders need to build toward Eucharistic participation throughout all their youth ministry efforts. Leaders need to ask themselves how they can support youth in prayer participation through silence, song, shared prayer, posture, and listening. Equally, ministry leaders need to be intentional about including programs and strategies that offer young people the opportunity to participate in discussion, demonstration, and hands-on experiences of prayer. Attentiveness to prayer then becomes the agenda for preparing youth for liturgy.

Participating in communal prayer and worship experiences deepens youth's personal prayer life while connecting them to the Eucharistic community. It is not uncommon, though, for different parts of the country and different parishes to have a unique spirituality. However, all forms of communal prayer can speak to young people when done well. "The Liturgy of the Hours, liturgies of reconciliation and healing, and ritual devotions such as the stations of the cross allow for creativity and adaptation to the life issues and cultural expressions of youth" (*From Age to Age*, no. 60).

Youth ministers must also help to foster a personal prayer life for each young person. *Renewing the Vision* says that "the symbols and rituals of liturgy become more meaningful for young people when they draw from their experiences of private prayer. Likewise, private prayer is revitalized by meaningful experiences of the liturgy" (p. 45). Helping young people develop their individual prayer life will only strengthen the gift they will bring back to the greater community.

The Church's rich sacramental life also has both a communal and a personal dimension. Participating in the sacraments is an integral part of Catholic identity. Providing opportunities for the sacrament of reconciliation on retreats and at different times during the year, fostering participation in the Eucharistic liturgy, and providing effective catechesis on each of the sacraments deepens both personal and communal worship.

Effective strategies for the component of prayer and worship include these:

- Pray, pray, pray.
  - Ask a group of community members to pray for individual young people or for the youth ministry team, or for both, daily.
  - Develop a monthly prayer calendar that includes prayer requests pertaining to youth ministry for each day of the month.

- Invite the parish staff and the entire youth ministry team to spend time praying for God's guidance and direction in the parish's ministry efforts with the young.
- Promote prayer within all ministry efforts and events with youth.
  - Promote personal prayer life.
  - Bring a prayerful spirit to all ministry.
  - Enable young people to plan and lead prayer. An effective ministry leader allows others to enter into the mission of prayer.
  - Offer prayers at key times during ministry events (in other words, at meals, before traveling, when someone is injured, upon safe return).
- Build time in youth ministry for silence, symbol, and ritual.
- Include music and song throughout youth ministry to invite youth to sing their prayers in liturgy.
- Support parents by advocating and preparing young people for participation in liturgy.
- Bring the Sunday readings into a young person's life during the week.
  - Utilize prayer forms such as *lectio divina*.
  - Utilize themes from Sunday readings for gatherings during the week and for retreats.
  - Provide resources that help youth and their families prepare for liturgy at home.
- Provide intentional preparation for youth participation in liturgy.
  - Encourage catechesis on the liturgy from the presider, or conduct sessions after the liturgy to "unpack" its content and meaning.
  - Invite someone knowledgeable about liturgy and the history of the worship space to give youth a tour of the church. The tour leader can familiarize youth with worship space and symbols.
  - Create a retreat that focuses on the pattern and elements of Mass.
  - Promote participation in liturgy in different cultural and ethnic parishes and communities.
  - Participate in liturgies with youth and take time for discussion before and after the liturgy.
- Provide large-group communal prayer experiences.

Praying together has a power and dynamic different from that of praying privately. Communal prayer teaches us lessons we cannot learn alone. It is an opportunity for mutual support in faith, hope, and love—a time to celebrate together who we are and whose we are.

The Liturgy: Source and Summit of Faith

Liturgy and Young People

> As youth ministers and advocates, we want all youth to know that the church does not just expect them to attend the liturgy, but in the Spirit of Christ, invites them to join us in giving thanks and praise. We need their enthusiasm and adventurous spirit to make our worship more fully alive. The whole community needs to accept full responsibility for the liturgy, and we invite youth to gather with us and take their rightful place in the church's worship life.[12] (*From Age to Age*, no. 10)

Young people are as much a part of the Church as adults. When it comes to belonging, the Church is one. It is not a "Church" of adults and then the "future Church" of youth. By the very nature of Catholic theology, all followers must stand before God together in the liturgy, old and young alike. The goal is for parishes to be truly Eucharistic communities. Although the Eucharist is broken, poured, and shared, it remains one loaf and one cup. Likewise, the members of the Body of Christ are one. In Christ there is no distinction between young and old. Communities that recognize this reality genuinely welcome young people into the regular worship life of the Church and create opportunities for young people to use their gifts in liturgy.

The liturgy should be the place where all come together, rather than a cause of disunity. The Catholic Church has always sought to be broad enough to encompass "people of every race, language and way of life" (see Eucharistic Prayer for Reconciliation, II). It is a Church that embraces a wide variety of styles and spiritualities and customs and opinions. No matter what our background or preferences may be, the liturgy is the place where we must be able to embrace one another.

Fully Conscious and Active Participation

Vatican II, in the *Constitution on the Sacred Liturgy*, says that "fully conscious and active participation" by all the faithful is the "right and duty" of all the faithful because of their Baptism (no. 14). Yet it has taken more than three decades for those profound insights to begin to take hold. Most of us were satisfied to look for something less than what was intended; we were happy when a parish had good singing and when lector and Communion ministries were done well. But good singing and good ministry are not enough for the young (nor should it be enough for anyone). The ministry of prayer and worship should be aimed toward the kind of participation the council called "fully conscious and active."

"Greater youth participation in the liturgy will not occur without an *intentional* effort to seek and encourage it[13]" (*From Age to Age*, no. 12). Following are the characteristics necessary for "fully conscious and active" participation.

Intergenerational

The presence and involvement of young people at *all* parish liturgies is a gift to the entire community. Ministry leaders must involve youth in authentic ways and avoid isolating young people in only one particular community liturgy. Fully conscious and active participation in the parish liturgical life, rather than token or segregated involvement, is integral to fostering the communal faith identity of young people.

Diversity

Respect for cultures and inclusion of local art, music, and expression should be visible. Ministry leaders need to be familiar with the diversity of races, cultures, and ages of those present in the assembly. The prayers, songs, and symbols need to be prepared knowing that the Church does "respect and foster the genius and talents of the various races and peoples" (*Constitution on the Sacred Liturgy*, no. 37).

Parish Commitment

If leadership of the parish is the least bit ambivalent about engaging teens in liturgical participation and ministries, it will fail in its attempt. The commitment begins with the pastoral team, especially the pastor. Parish leaders must articulate to the parish their commitment and vision for youth involvement as an important first step.

Listen to Youth

Listening is fundamental. Identifying specific needs of young people should be balanced by seeking ideas from other identifiable groups. Youth needs and concerns are often not different from other parishioners' needs.

Music

Singing is the sign of the heart's joy and the heart's lament. Singing is important for a sense of celebration. At every liturgy the music needs to be singable and prayable, with strong text and lyrics. Musical choices should be determined by how well the music will be accepted by the assembly and how well the music will uplift and empower the liturgy. The goal is to bring about an understanding that the assembly does not sing *at* the liturgy, but rather *sings the liturgy.*

Visually Dynamic Symbols and Actions

"Today's youth have been educated through multimedia. Their visual sense is their primary way of learning and responding to their environment" (*From Age to Age*, no. 69). Youth can become bored (so too can the entire assembly) when the visual nature of liturgy is weak. The *Constitution on the Sacred Liturgy* calls for "signs perceptible to the senses" (no. 7). This principle challenges parishes to make the signs and symbols of liturgy shout, through the preparation of the environment and the planning for participation in the prayers and actions of liturgy.

Proclamation of the Word

When young people and adults take time to prepare and proclaim the readings well, the community will be more engaged in listening to the particular proclamations.

Homilies

Without fail, the one part of the Mass about which the entire congregation has an opinion is the homily. Ministry leaders should influence the homily by insisting that the homilist addresses the real-life concerns of young people. Young people respond to a priest who helps them understand the relevance of the Gospel in their lives today.

Liturgy Planning

Young people have much to offer in regard to helping plan liturgies. Parishes should have youth representatives on their liturgy committees to advocate for the youth of the parish and to give a youthful perspective to planning. *General Instruction of the Roman Missal* is essential for everyone working on planning liturgies. The Eucharistic liturgy is the universal offering and celebration of God's salvation in Jesus Christ. The liturgy, because of its universality, must be able both to express the faith of people from many cultures throughout the world and to develop a sense of unity in the celebration. *General Instruction of the Roman Missal* is the "how to" book for the liturgy, providing both norms for unity with Catholics throughout the world and allowances for local customs and expressions.

Ministry of Hospitality

"Parishes . . . can focus on the hospitality provided at liturgy, encourage young people to attend liturgy with their friends, build a sense of community among young people prior to liturgy, minister in a personal way, and affirm the presence of young people whenever possible" (*Renewing the Vision*, p. 47). The vibrancy that youth add to the liturgy is a great sign of hope for the community. Young people can have an impact by creating a sense of welcome for all community members regardless of age.

Special Commissionings and Blessings

Liturgy has a special impact when an occasional focus is put on the youth of the faith community. Special commissionings or blessings during Mass as young people prepare to depart for retreats, work camps, and diocesan or national youth conferences contribute to youth's connection to the parish. Special blessings for graduates or young people leaving for college signify that the community recognizes those important aspects of their lives.

Prayers of the Faithful

Inviting young people to contribute to the community's Prayers of the Faithful and to include their special events or occasions in those prayers deepens the connection between the community's liturgy and their world.

Ministry Mentors

Young people need adults to mentor and apprentice them. It goes without saying that young people, as well as adults, are likely to participate more fully and with greater ease if they are secure in their liturgical roles. In that way they will be empowered as young leaders and ministers—and as faith-filled worshipers.

Liturgical Catechesis

It is regrettable that ministry often neglects forming the assembly. The goal of liturgical catechesis is to "promote an active, conscious, and genuine participation in the liturgy of the Church" (*General Directory*, no. 25). "A major barrier however is a lack of understanding of the sacramental symbols and rituals. . . . A specific objective of intentional catechesis for liturgy is to assist teens through reflection and sharing in exploring how liturgical symbols and rituals celebrate their experiences of God and life events[14]" (*From Age to Age*, no. 39). This also means assisting young people in becoming familiar with the liturgical documents.

Liturgical Mindset

Full participation begins long before Sunday Mass. Therefore Mass is not just one more thing on a young person's "must do" list. Instilling in young people such habits as looking over the Scriptures, fasting until Mass, or not distracting themselves in the early hours of Sunday help them come to Mass mindful of their responsibility—to themselves, one another, and God. Just as they want the priest, choir, and lector to prepare, young people also must prepare to be good members of the assembly. Families as well will enter more fully into the Eucharistic celebration when they are encouraged to pray in the home as a family.

Conclusion

The writing of *From Age to Age* was prompted by the belief that gathering for worship is central to the life of all believers. However, many young people seem to be missing at the table. Without their presence, the Church misses the special gift of enthusiasm and vitality that young people can bring to the larger community. The 1997 publication of *From Age to Age* prompted ordained, pastoral, and liturgical ministers to gather together with young people to discuss its message. Out of that dialogue came insights, strategies, and a renewed commitment to creating vibrant prayer and worship for and with young people. This chapter reflects the fruit of those discussions.

Engaging young people in the prayer and worship life of the Church is the responsibility of the entire faith community. And there are certainly varied perspectives about the best way to achieve that goal. Those involved in liturgical, catechetical, family, and youth ministries must see themselves as partners in this noble adventure.

Chapter Questions

1. How does your parish's ministry of prayer and worship incorporate young people into the sacramental life of the Church?
2. Identify three ways your faith community involves young people in liturgy.
3. Identify three ways to more fully integrate young people into the community's worship.
4. What opportunities are offered in your community for young people to develop and experience communal and personal prayer?
5. Describe the difference between informational prayer experiences and transformational prayer experiences.

Chapter 13

Youth Ministry: The Family Dimension

Randy Raus with Leif Kehrwald

Introduction

Parents remain the single most influential people in the lives of teenagers. Ministry to families is critical to the value of youth ministry in a parish. It can be a mistaken assumption by ministry leaders to think that any ministry apart from the family will be enough to foster deep-seated commitment and transformation in the lives of young people. Parents are the principal youth ministers and catechists of their family. Youth ministry leaders must work in union with parents to provide an environment where young people's social, emotional, and spiritual growth is nurtured.

Objectives

This chapter situates the family as an integral dimension in a comprehensive approach to youth ministry, provides practical strategies, and describes the common obstacles to family ministry.

A Christian Vision of Family Life

The Christian family is holy and sacred. This is a simple but profound statement that carries far-reaching implications for the Church and all believers. Interestingly, most believers would not hesitate to affirm the truth of that statement. Something about living in a family, even amid its foibles and quirks and problems and dysfunction, reveals a sort of wholesome sacredness. Most of the time we cannot explain it, but we know it is there.

Holy and sacred does not mean problem-free—not by any means. All it means is that we are believers and that we have occasionally encountered the Mystery of love.

The family is holy and sacred not by pure happenstance. The family must ascent to belief and faith, intentionally pursuing God's presence, which lingers among the ordinary and extraordinary events of family life. However weak and imperfect, intentionality is key.

It is one thing for families themselves to acknowledge the sacredness of family life and quite another matter for the Church to theologically say so, but that is just what the Church has done.

Pope Leo XIII declared that "the family was ordained of God. . . . It was before the church, or rather the first form of the church on earth" (Mitch Finley, "Family Orphaned by the Church," in *National Catholic Reporter,* February 28, 1986, pp. 11–12). More recently, in his book *Sacraments and Sacramentality,* theologian Bernard Cooke says, "The Christian family is meant to be the most basic instance of Christian community, people bonded together by their shared relationship to the risen Jesus" (p. 92).

Popes Paul VI and John Paul II have also affirmed the sacred nature of the Christian family. In *On the Church in the Modern World (Evangelii Nuntiandi),* his apostolic exhortation on evangelization, Pope Paul VI said, "There should be found in every Christian family the various aspects of the entire Church" (no. 71).

In his exhortation on the family, *Familiaris Consortio,* Pope John Paul II states, "Among the fundamental tasks of the Christian family is its ecclesial task: the family is placed at the service of building up the Kingdom of God in history by participating in the life and mission of the Church" (no. 49). The Holy Father goes on to say that "the Christian family also builds up the Kingdom of God in history through the everyday realities that concern and distinguish its state of life" (no. 50). In developing that theme, Pope John Paul II, drawing on the teaching of Vatican II and Pope Paul VI, stresses that the specific conjugal love of spouses, the love meant to be expressed in their lives and extended through their family and children to the community in which they live, is what "constitute[s] the nucleus of the saving mission of the Christian family in the Church and for the Church" (no. 50).

In their 1994 pastoral message to families, *Follow the Way of Love,* the U.S. Catholic bishops state quite profoundly the Church's teaching on family:

> A family is our first community and most basic way, in which the Lord gathers us, forms us and acts in the world. The early Church expressed this truth by calling the Christian family a *domestic church* or *church of the home.* (P. 8)

This marvelous teaching was underemphasized for centuries, but reintroduced by the Second Vatican Council. The point of the teaching is simple yet profound. Today we are still uncovering its rich treasure.

Ministry leaders must give serious thought and reflection to this statement:

> As Christian families, you not only belong to the church, but your daily life is a true expression of the church. Your domestic church is not complete by itself, of course. It should be united with and supported by parishes and other communities within the larger church. Christ has called you and joined you to himself in and through the sacraments. Therefore, you share in one and the same mission that he gives to the whole church. (*Follow the Way of Love*, p. 8)

Notice what the bishops did *not* say. They did not say, "As Christian families, when you say your meal prayers, . . . when you gather around the Advent wreath, . . . when you worship at Mass, that's a true expression of Church. Of course all those are true expressions, but the bishops use the term "your daily life." Because you are a believer, because you seek God's presence in your normal activities, your *daily life* as a family is a true expression of Church. These teachings recognize the redemptive power of a God who loves so fully and unconditionally that holiness and sacredness are unconditionally available.

As Mitch and Kathy Finley say, "*Family spirituality* means no more and no less than this: A family's ongoing attempts to live every dimension of its life in communion with the Cross and Resurrection of Jesus the Christ" (*Building Christian Families*, p. 18). They also recognize the important relationship between the Church of the home and the Church of the parish, saying: "The local parish and the universal church depend upon families for their fundamental vitality as they strive to make Christ present in the modern world. It also means that as families go, so goes the church. If we want a strong church in the future, we must pay attention to family life in the church today" (p. 16).

The Christian vision of family life speaks about the family as a community of life and love. It proclaims that family life is sacred and that family activities are holy, that God's love is revealed and communicated in new ways each and every day through Christian families. This Christian vision of family life calls families to a unique identity and mission. The Christian family *is* holy and sacred. As a result families can come to believe that God dwells among them, and so they respond to God's gracious activity in their lives.

Families and Faith

In their book *The Search for Common Ground: What Unites and Divides Catholic Americans*, James D. Davidson and his Purdue University colleagues acknowledge that family religious practice is a key predictor of a young person's adult faith practice. They report the conclusions from a rather extensive study of the beliefs and religious activity of both practicing and nonpracticing Catholics. Catholic parishioners were surveyed throughout the United States and interviewed across the state of Indiana. Generally the research highlights the importance of certain factors in establishing an adult commitment to faith. Those factors point toward pastoral initiatives, such as fostering a healthy home life, early childhood experiences, and a good religious education. With respect to family and parental influence, Davidson and his colleagues summarized the research findings as follows:

> Family upbringing variables have a strong effect on the respondents' tendency, as adults, to accept traditional Catholic beliefs and practices and to agree with the Church on sexual and reproductive ethics. The strongest predictor of a high score on both of these indices is the respondent's level of childhood religiosity: respondents who report frequent Mass attendance, Communion, and prayer as children are over eight times more likely to report high levels of traditional beliefs and practices today. . . . Respondents who were close to their parents or whose parents frequently talked to them about religion are twice as likely to report high levels of traditional beliefs and practices than those who were not close to their parents or whose parents "rarely" or "never" talked about religion. (Pp. 98–99)

The factor with the most impact on Catholics' religious beliefs and practices is *childhood religiosity,* which is nurtured through the family and parish or school religious education.

Davidson's family upbringing study is corroborated by a Search Institute study involving mainline Protestant denominations, which found that the three most important factors that empower faith maturity among young people are family based. Faith maturity is a young person's ability to say yes to his or her beliefs, own them, and act on them by his or her own choice. The research also shows that without the following three key formative experiences *in the home,* genuine faith maturity is harder to come by:

- *Family faith conversations.* Hearing their parents' faith stories is one of the most important influences on the faith of children and teenagers. Open-ended discussions on relevant and controversial issues create an atmosphere for dialogue and growth. Although it is important for parents to know just where their teen stands on a given issue, it is just as important for parents to allow for a variety of opinions. It is also helpful when parents are willing to share times of doubt and questioning in their own faith journey. Sharing the rough points can create new opportunities for conversation and understanding.
- *Family ritual and devotions.* This activity moves from informal conversation to something a bit more structured and intentional. People who regularly have family devotions, prayer, or Bible reading at home tend to have higher faith maturity. Families who take some time to reflect on their daily, weekly, and seasonal habits will likely discover some opportunities for family ritual.
- *Family outreach and service.* Faced with so many problems of their own, many families are not motivated to serve others. Yet often acts of selfless mercy can transform woes into healing, as well as bring help to those who are in greater need. The most powerful influence on faith and family unity is working together to help others. One sure way to gain a world vision and a desire to serve others is to invite people who represent issues in the world to visit and perhaps share a meal.

(Adapted from "Building Strong Families Fact Sheet:
A Preliminary Study from YMCA/Search Institute
on What Parents Need to Succeed")

God seeks a relationship with every family. Therefore, families are called to respond to God's graciousness. The free gift of God's love is always available, but when people intentionally respond to God's overtures, they find themselves in a sacramental relationship with the Creator.

The Family Dimension

The effective ministry leader sees the family dimension of ministry as a way to successfully take ministry to a more comprehensive level. *Renewing the Vision* states, "One of the most important tasks for the Church today is to promote the faith growth of families by encouraging families to share, celebrate, and live their faith at home and in the world" (p. 12).

A study commissioned by Saint Mary's Press shows that the youth ministry leader of today understands the need for partnership with parents ("Youth Ministry: Attitudes and Opinions," CMMS, 2000). The study showed that the top-ranked need for youth ministry resources is on the topic of parents' understanding and being involved in adolescent faith development. The fifth-ranked need for resources is on the topic of exploring family-based youth ministry. The field of youth ministry has evolved into a more collaborative process involving parents, families, and other ministry and community efforts that impact the lives of teens. An effective parish youth ministry model starts with a family ministry element as one of the cornerstones of youth ministry within the parish community.

Get to Know the Family Structure

The United States bishops, in the document *Renewing the Vision*, state:

> We are also concerned about the consequences of the social and economic forces affecting today's families. The effects of consumerism and the entertainment media often encourage a

culture of isolation. Far too many families lack sufficient time together and the resources to develop strong family relationships, to communicate life-giving values and a religious faith, to celebrate family rituals, to participate in family activities, and to contribute to the well-being of their community. (P. 5)

In an attempt to articulate the Christian vision of family life, the Church cannot ignore the cultural reality in which the family lives. In fact, without a solid understanding of the pressures and struggles that families face each day, most of what we have to say about the holy and sacred nature of family life will appear largely irrelevant to most families.

Today's family is not what we were raised to believe it should be. Today's American family is bombarded by opportunities, challenges, expectations, and distractions from all fronts. Most families cannot keep pace with the rapid growth and change of today's society. Although it is filled with attractive opportunities, much of what society offers is ultimately detrimental to healthy and faith-full family living.

The U.S. Census Bureau reports that just over 70 percent of American families with children ages twelve to seventeen have only one child. The percentage of those same families that have three or more children is a mere 4.4 percent ("America's Families and Living Arrangements, March 2000," *www.census.gov/population/socdemo/hh-fam/p20-537/2000/tabF1.txt*). In 2000 nearly 27 percent of American children were living in single-parent homes ("American Association for Single People," *www.singlesrights.com/main.html*). And keep in mind that a lot of "single parenting" occurs in two-parent homes. Also, many parents parent better, and their children thrive better, in a single-parent setting than in a home where the parents are highly contentious toward each other.

Another notable factor in families today is the high percentage of families where both parents are employed outside the home. Statistics also show an increasing delay in marriage and child rearing, which means that parents of teens today are older than parents of teens in previous decades (FamilyEducation.com Web site, *www.familyeducation.com/home*).

As we explore the holy and sacred nature of family life, we cannot ignore the social reality of family struggle and strife. Families do not live in isolation, but rather in a complicated and confusing society. The Church loses its sense of relevance for parents and families only when it ignores those realities.

When Church leaders recognize the realities and the tremendous efforts that many families make just to cope, then families begin to find an ally in their local Church community and can more readily see how to pursue their faith amid all the other demands and expectations of life. With practical, pastoral understanding from the parish community, families can begin to see how faith becomes interwoven into the fabric of their busy lives and not just view it as an added set of activities and obligations. When that integration occurs, families have no trouble recognizing their holy and sacred nature.

Parish and Families in Partnership

When it comes to empowering young people to live as disciples of Jesus Christ in the world today, both the home and the parish have the same tasks:

- to teach and model the Catholic faith in a personal and dialogical manner
- to encourage genuine spiritual growth through exposure to prayer, liturgy, retreats, and other Catholic rituals
- to engage in works of mercy and acts of justice for those who are poor and disenfranchised

Connecting with families isn't one more job in youth ministry—it is part of a ministry that supports everything done on behalf of young people. It can take time, effort, and resources, but the connections pay off in serving youth and strengthening a parish's youth ministry.

For many youth ministers, their love for young people has drawn them into youth ministry. That's terrific, but *parents and families must not be left behind.* As unpredictable and sometimes difficult as it can be to work with parents and families, youth ministers need them as partners in youth ministry. When the parish and the family work together on the tasks listed above, even greater good occurs. These practical suggestions help facilitate that partnership:

- Share the vision for comprehensive youth ministry. Discuss the idea of partnership.
- Use all available communication channels to keep parents and families informed about the youth ministry program.
- Help parents of adolescents experience Church as being "on their side"; that is, show them that the parish wants the same things for their youth as they do.
- Learn more about family life.
- Connect the parents of adolescents with one another as resources and for support.
- Build a bridge between youth ministry involvement and the home by giving parents information and resources that reinforce the content and activities in which their youth are involved.
- Provide ideas and resources that families can use at home.
- Provide ways for parents to help with special events and activities, such as service trips, retreats, and youth liturgies.
- Provide tips, ideas, and lots of encouragement to parents to help them communicate with their teens about what the teens are learning and discussing in youth ministry.
- Make home visits or spend time with families before or after Mass or during parish events.
- Host workshops on effective parenting.
- Encourage family dialogue by organizing family retreats, family faith-sharing gatherings, and the like.
- Encourage family involvement in justice and service work.
- Develop small weekly or monthly faith-sharing groups for parents.
- Create parent call lists and e-mail lists to help parents connect.
- Plan family intentional activities, like father-daughter dances, mother-son picnics, and combined catechetical events that invite both teens and parents to attend.
- Ensure that all youth and parish ministry programs are family friendly.
- Remember the power of prayer.

The Gift of Families

Families give a gift back to the parish by improving the well-being of the community. Families can be inspiration to other families and to young people themselves. In parishes we often observe families that convey a true love for one another and God. That type of love shows, and it also is contagious. Strong families often give young people who come from disconnected families an example and a model for a strong family.

Parents are helped by communities that support them and affirm the gifts they bring. Therefore affirmation should be a consistent aspect of ministry with families. Strategies for affirming parents and families include these:

- Write notes of affirmation to parents when you see their child do something extraordinary.
- Invite parents whose lives are daily expressions of a solid Christian family to share their gifts and help other families by serving as youth leaders or parent leaders.
- Acknowledge important family celebrations like wedding anniversaries.
- Take the time to tell parents how amazing their children are.
- Take the time to tell young people how great their parents are.
- Never criticize teens to their parents or parents to their teens.
- Organize times when the community can pray for parents and families.
- Mobilize parents to pray for their teenagers.
- Encourage young people to write letters of affirmation to their parents and parents to write letters of encouragement to their children.
- Create opportunities for young people to experience their parents in a different setting.
- Sit with parents at their children's events.
- Provide resources to parents to help them pray with their family.

Obstacles to Family Ministry

It is relatively easy for parents of young people to intimidate youth workers; after all, some youth ministers are young and don't have children of their own. It can be difficult to completely relate to what a parent of a teenager is going through until you have been the parent of a teenager. Youth ministry leaders must not allow a lack of experience or others' perceptions to distract them from ministering to families. It is also important that youth ministers realize that sometimes they can be seen as a threat to the relationship parents have with their teen; parents can feel that they are not as "cool" or as in tune as you are with their child. Realize that those thoughts and emotions are normal. Consider the following guidelines:

- To build trust with parents, always use an open-door approach to ministry that invites parents to participate and observe youth events and meetings. The ministry professional should always be available to meet with parents and families.
- Ministry leaders should never try to be something they are not. Admitting that one's knowledge is limited in some area and admitting the need for ongoing education is the sign of a well-formed and healthy minister. It also communicates the need to partner more closely with parents, who indeed know their own children best.
- The ministry leader may love the teens she or he works with, but remembering that their parents love them more is essential. The love between a parent and her or his children should never be taken for granted.
- Involving parents in ministry leadership can ease parental concerns about their child's involvement in ministry programs and events. Having parents in leadership roles will also provide an ongoing reminder of the need to keep ministry family friendly.
- Continually conveying the idea of working in "partnership" with parents helps promote a willingness to recognize the role of the parent in the life of the young person.

"Every effort should be made to strengthen and develop pastoral care for the family, which should be treated as a real matter of priority, in the certainty that future evangelization depends largely on the domestic Church" (*Familiaris Consortio*, no. 65). To maintain a joyful family requires much from both the parents and the children. Each member of the family has to become, in a special way, the servant of the others. Youth ministry leaders are called to foster this type of relationship with families.

Conclusion

Family life is the first and most formative experience of acceptance and belonging along life's journey. It is our first experience of community. When the family connects with the community of the Church, the family becomes the Church of the home. In a homily given in Perth, Australia, on November 30, 1986, Pope John Paul II made the following statement:

> "The family is the domestic church." The meaning of this traditional Christian idea is that the home is the Church in miniature. The Church is the sacrament of God's love. She is a communion of faith and life. She is a mother and teacher. She is at the service of the whole human family as it goes forward towards its ultimate destiny. In the same way the family is a community of life and love. It educates and leads its members to their full human maturity and it serves the good of all along the road of life. . . . In its own way it is a living image and historical representation of the mystery of the Church. The future of the world and of the Church, therefore, passes through the family. ("Pastoral Visit in Australia," *Homily of John Paul II*, no. 3)

This papal teaching reinforces the challenge to recognize the family as an authentic expression of the Church of the home. All parish ministries and programs must recognize the unique ministry of the family and must search for ways to partner with families.

Chapter Questions

1. On a scale of one to ten, ten being the highest, how aware are parents of the vision and scope of the youth ministry program in your parish? What would foster their awareness?
2. What one strategy could be utilized to build relationships with the parents of the young people in your parish or school?
3. Identify one strategy that might be implemented to involve parents more fully in your parish youth ministry program.
4. What is the prevailing parish staff attitude about, or approach to, families?
5. What strategy can the parish utilize to remind families that they are "holy and sacred"?
6. How can youth ministry partner with families in fostering the faith of young people?

Chapter 14

Youth Ministry: The Multicultural Dimension

Anne-Marie Yu-Phelps

Introduction

The Church is a multicultural Church, and youth ministry should reflect that in an intentional way. We are multicultural not only in the sense of race, ethnicity, and nationality but also in terms of gender, class, sexual orientation, able-bodiedness, and age. We are young and old, poor and rich, gay and straight, female and male, disabled and able, and we are present in every continent on Earth. Our faith tradition is enriched by this diversity of people and the many gifts brought forth by those of us who come from such different backgrounds and perspectives.

Objectives

This chapter illustrates the need for diversity in youth ministry strategies and programming that reflects the multicultural nature of the global Church, and strategies and ideas for how to achieve that goal.

A Multicultural Perspective

In *Renewing the Vision* three primary goals are set forth for ministry with adolescents; in all three goals, it is important to be attentive to the multicultural dimension of ministry. Goal one is "to empower young people to live as disciples of Jesus Christ in our world today" (p. 9). Jesus was a model of inclusion and acceptance for all; he was particularly welcoming of those who are traditionally marginalized by society—the sick, the disabled, the poor and oppressed, women and children, the aged, ethnic minorities— and we must do likewise if we are to live as Jesus's disciples.

Goal two is "to draw young people to responsible participation in the life, mission, and work of the Catholic faith community" (p. 11). To participate responsibly, young people must first feel comfortable within the Catholic faith community, and they must feel like it is *their* community. For those who are not traditionally part of the mainstream culture, efforts need to be made to make them feel welcomed and included as full-fledged members of the community, not as some special but separate segment of the community.

Goal three is "to foster the total personal and spiritual growth of each young person" (p. 15). To meet that need for all adolescents, we must nurture them in a way that allows them to grow comfortable with their own identity in all its facets, including their race and ethnicity, gender, sexual orientation, gifts, and limitations. Because adolescence is a time when young people experience tremendous tension in their desire to both conform and individuate, it is particularly important to pay attention to the different aspects of their identity development.

Beware and Be Aware

The Catholic Tradition calls us to be inclusive and to recognize and celebrate the inherent human dignity of all people. Although we share a common humanity, however, there is a danger in falling into the mindset that "we are all really the same." That mindset does not take into account cultural differences and the impact of those differences on a young person's identity development, faith practice, social relationships, and so forth. Taken to an extreme, that mindset can be arrogant and abusive, and it can be used in an unconsciously oppressive manner. It is particularly important for the dominant culture to be aware of the danger because it can be taken for granted that the dominant culture is the norm and everything else is something "other." Members of the dominant culture often learn to function within that culture without necessarily ever needing to learn otherwise; outsiders to the dominant culture grow up learning how to negotiate life by both holding onto their own native culture and functioning and adapting to the dominant culture in order to survive. Tensions often arise when there is a direct conflict between the teaching and practices of a native culture and the dominant culture. Adolescents who are working on their own identity development are particularly vulnerable to those tensions and need as much genuine support and affirmation as possible. All teens need to be assured that regardless of culture or differences, they are created in God's image and loved unconditionally and that they are viewed as full and equal members of the community; those assurances must be modeled, not merely spoken.

Virgilio Elizondo captures that importance well in writing, "To promote the emergence of a real multicultural religious experience, we must go from a benevolent tolerance of the otherness of the others to a sincere reverence of others in their otherness" (Barbara Wilkerson, ed., *Multicultural Religious Education,* pp. 397–398). Achieving "sincere reverence" requires not only sensitivity and awareness but also an active effort on the part of those who work with youth to educate themselves about other cultures—particularly those represented by the youth with whom they work.

On the opposite end of the spectrum, it is important not to go overboard in an effort to be culturally sensitive, because adolescents are experts at sensing tokenism and hypocrisy. Young people who are part of a traditionally marginalized culture are often put in the position of acting as the spokesperson or "expert" for their particular group, and that is an unfair position in which to put anyone. For one thing, it implies a lack of awareness that even within specific cultural groups, there exists a diversity of viewpoints, traditions, practices, and beliefs. It also denies a young person his or her own sense of individuality within the cultural group, and it puts an undue pressure on young people to represent their culture in a way that those who are part of the dominant culture are never called on to do. The danger of stereotyping also falls into this category; by placing someone in the position of spokesperson or expert, a tendency exists to generalize that person's understanding or experience and apply it to a whole group of people as that group's cultural norm. Just as there is diversity in an individual's experience of the dominant culture, so there is diversity in an individual's experience of a traditionally marginalized culture.

In working to promote multiculturalism in youth ministry, it is also important to be aware of our own assumptions and biases. That self-awareness is critical in moving toward a genuine sensitivity that will enable us to achieve that desired "sincere reverence." According to Elizondo:

> Western theologians still tend to see the Western churches as "the Church," while viewing the churches of other people of

the world as "local churches." Western tradition is regarded as "Tradition," while everything else is regarded as local tradition. Western theologies are regarded simply as theology, while the theologies and methodologies of other cultures are regarded as ethnic or particular theologies. (P. 397)

If that is our operating assumption or bias, then a hierarchy is automatically established that sets up Western culture, tradition, and theology as the dominant and primary culture, tradition, and theology, and relegates all others to a secondary or inferior position. If that is the lens through which we view the world, then how is that assumption going to translate into our interactions with youth who are not part of the Western culture and tradition? Only when we can identify our own assumptions and biases are we able to move forward in overcoming them; that enables us to be more empathetic in understanding the perspectives and struggles of those who come from a background different from our own and breaks down any notion of hierarchical ranking of views or traditions as primary or secondary.

Awareness, Understanding, Affirmation, and Empowerment

In describing a comprehensive vision of youth ministry, *Renewing the Vision* specifically calls on ministries to be multicultural. It states, "Ministry with adolescents is multicultural when it focuses on a specialized ministry to youth of particular racial and ethnic cultures *and* promotes multicultural awareness among all youth" (p. 22). We can take that definition one step further to include not only race and ethnicity but also cultures related to gender, sexual orientation, socio-economic class, learning styles, and physical and cognitive abilities. If we focus on race and ethnicity only, we exclude youth who come from a number of other traditionally marginalized cultures who need just as much attention and support as those who come from racial or ethnic cultures that are traditionally ignored, because those other elements are also critical aspects of one's identity. One of the key elements of the quotation, however, is the importance of promoting multicultural awareness among all youth. Even if a youth ministry program is homogeneous in some of the elements of a young person's identity, it is unlikely that it will be homogeneous in all those elements:

> All ministry with adolescents needs to incorporate ethnic traditions, values, and rituals into ministerial programming; teach about the variety of ethnic cultures in the Catholic Church; provide opportunities for cross-cultural experiences; and foster acceptance and respect for cultural diversity. . . . Ministry with adolescents needs to counteract prejudice, racism, and discrimination by example, with youth themselves becoming models of fairness and nondiscrimination. (*Renewing the Vision*, p. 23)

Promoting those goals among all youth (as well as their parents and the adults who work with youth) will enable all young people to feel like valued and respected members of the community. It will also equip them to function respectfully and reverently in other areas of their life where they might encounter more people who come from backgrounds or experiences different from their own.

Models for Ministry

How might those goals be accomplished? How do we empower *all* young women and men to be comfortable with who they are and to be leaders in the Church and in the world? How do we help to foster "a sincere reverence of others in their otherness"? Following are some examples of program models that have been successful.

A parish youth ministry group learns about the social injustices suffered by young people in East Timor. They educate themselves about the issues and make contact with the local diocese in East Timor, expressing a desire to be in solidarity with their youth. E-mail contact is established, and the youth begin to exchange prayer requests, promising to pray for and support one another in their respective struggles. Meanwhile, the young people who started this project visit neighboring parishes and Catholic schools to raise awareness of the injustices being suffered by the East Timorese. The prayer net is widened and awareness is raised. Government and Church leaders are contacted in an effort to advocate for those youth. A cultural exchange is arranged. After several years the people of East Timor experience liberation and the young people who started this project feel proud to have played a small role in providing support, solidarity, advocacy, and prayer for their friends who live on the other side of the world. Not only did this project teach about another culture and provide a limited crosscultural experience, it also empowered the youth to recognize the role they can play in social-justice issues. It emphasized the global nature of the Church and the fact that we are called to make a preferential option for the poor and vulnerable, to show solidarity to others, and to recognize the inherent right of all people to dignity and life.

A Catholic girls' school that believes in the importance of empowering young women to take on leadership roles in the Church incorporates into its religion curriculum a unit on homiletics. As a final exam, each student must choose a Gospel passage and deliver a homily to her classmates. Having been formally trained in this way, students who have completed the course are then invited to take their skill beyond the classroom. Each week during the school's celebration of the liturgy of the word, a different student is invited to give a reflection on the Gospel passage of the day. Offering a chapel reflection enables them to share a part of their faith with their school community. It also enables them to experience first-hand a leadership role in ministry that is not usually afforded to young people in general and to young women in particular.

A predominantly white suburban parish partners with an urban parish composed of young people of color to plan a retreat together. Representatives from each parish plan a series of meetings over the next several months to get to know one another and plan the specifics of the retreat. When the retreat is launched, it includes a large number of adolescents from both parishes who are eager for this crosscultural experience. During the retreat the young people are able to interact and dialogue with peers from a background very different from their own. They engage in community building, prayer experiences, faith-sharing activities, conversations about race and racism, as well as a social-dance. They are able to break down stereotypes and learn to recognize that despite their differences in such social barriers as race, ethnicity, and class, they share many aspects of youth culture. They are also able to experience the *"unity* in diversity that characterizes the universal Church" (*Renewing the Vi-*

sion, p. 23). After the retreat both parishes express a desire to continue the partnership through other follow-up activities.

A Catholic school sponsors a student organization that addresses the issue of discrimination toward and harassment of gay and lesbian youth and provides support and solidarity for students who have a same-sex orientation. Basing their mission statement on the United States bishops' pastoral letter *Always Our Children: A Pastoral Message to Parents of Homosexual Children and Suggestions for Pastoral Ministers,* the group is clear about their Catholic identity and is not about promoting sexual activity, but rather affirming young people who have a homosexual orientation (who, like all others, are also created in the image and likeness of God), reducing stereotyping of and discrimination toward homosexual people, and providing support to heterosexual students who have friends or family members of a same-sex orientation. The group hosts movies and discussions as well as speakers and activities that help the school community address issues such as homophobia and the use of derogatory language. It is their way of responding to the bishops' statement:

> The teachings of the Church make it clear that the fundamental human rights of homosexual persons must be defended and that all of us must strive to eliminate any forms of injustice, oppression, or violence against them (cf. *The Pastoral Care of Homosexual Persons,* 1986, no. 10). It is not sufficient only to avoid unjust discrimination. . . . The Christian community should offer its homosexual sisters and brothers understanding and pastoral care. (*Always Our Children*)

A U.S. Catholic church has a sister community in El Salvador. The Salvadoran village has a large youth population, and the youth of the U.S. church express a desire to send a youth delegation to visit the community and to dialogue specifically with the Salvadoran youth. The U.S. youth have previously participated in service trips to Appalachia and Chicago. They feel that having the opportunity to experience the culture of the rural poor as well as the urban poor has broadened their worldview; in their minds, a logical next step would be to continue to expand their crosscultural experiences by visiting a developing nation and learning about the issues and injustices suffered by their brothers and sisters in the Salvadoran community. As with their previous service trips, the youth going on the delegation to El Salvador carry out extensive fund-raising activities to help pay for the trip. They also participate in a series of orientation activities to build community among the group of adolescents and adults who will be undertaking the trip; to learn about the history, culture, and political climate of El Salvador; as well as to develop some basic Spanish language skills. While in El Salvador, the group from the U.S. community helps the Salvadoran community rebuild their village church, which had been destroyed. The adolescents of both communities participate in a series of meetings to discuss the similarities and differences of their respective youth cultures—topics such as education, dating, family relationships, and sports are all covered in those dialogues. A meeting is held with embassy officials at the U.S. embassy in San Salvador so that the delegation can advocate for their Salvadoran brothers and sisters. The young people return to the United States having further broadened their worldview through this crosscultural experience; they also become involved in raising awareness among the rest of their Church community and participating in advocacy activities on behalf of their Salvadoran sister community.

Young people from a variety of religious traditions come together to participate in a series of discussions and activities that enable them to break down stereotypes and learn about one another's faith traditions. Some of the activities include interfaith prayer services, an interfaith Thanksgiving dinner, guest speakers, and observing or participating in one another's worship services. In an era of increasing religious diversity in our nation, as well as increasing religious intolerance and religious wars around the world, those shared activities and dialogues enable the young people to develop respect and understanding for those who hold a different belief system. This responds to the bishops' assertion that "ministry with adolescents involves creating healthier civic communities for all young people . . . [and] involves networking with leaders in congregations of diverse faith traditions" (*Renewing the Vision*, p. 24).

A youth ministry program incorporates music, dance, prayers, art, language, and worship styles from all the different ethnic cultures represented by their youth. They are attentive to the fact that a variety of ethnicities exist within a particular race, so they do not presume that all Asian people, all Hispanic-Latino people, all Native

American people, all people of African descent, or all Anglo-Europeans share the same cultural traditions. Within the category of "white," for example, are Italians, Irish, Germans, and so forth, each with their own cultural traditions. Within the category of "Asian" are Chinese, Japanese, Filipinos, and so forth, each with *their* own cultural traditions. In this way celebrating diversity does not become something that "only people of color do." Rather, it is an acknowledgment and reverencing of *all* different ethnic traditions. It also addresses the bishops' call to make sure that worship services "reflect cultural diversity through the use of symbols, traditions, musical styles, and native language" (*Renewing the Vision*, p. 45).

These are but a sampling of program ideas that not only help all adolescents grow in their awareness and understanding of others but also affirm and empower those who are traditionally marginalized to take their place as full members of the community and leaders in the Church.

Teaching by Word and Example

Renewing the Vision makes clear the importance of multicultural programming for adolescents. Equally important is training adults who work with those youth and educating parents about multicultural issues. That is because "effective catechesis with youth requires that the adult members of our community grow continually in their faith and in their ability to share it with others. This growth is especially necessary for the parents of adolescents. We cannot expect more of youth than we do of adults. The ways we adults learn about, express, and live our faith is a vigorous support or a serious obstacle in effectively catechizing youth" (*The Challenge of Adolescent Catechesis*, p. 3). If the parents of an adolescent or the ministry leaders are not culturally sensitive or aware, it would be unreasonable to expect the adolescent to be culturally sensitive and aware. Thus, it is imperative to develop parent education programs as well as youth ministry training programs to meet those needs. Such programs should both raise awareness of multicultural issues and help adults develop sensitivity and comfort in addressing those issues with young people. Adults also need to model the kind of affirmation and inclusion—of "sincere reverence of others in their otherness"—that we expect of our youth. Only in that way can we teach our young people, by word and by example, how to function sensitively and compassionately in our ever more pluralistic society.

Conclusion

When adolescents think of the Church, the image that comes to mind should be one that is multicultural in the broadest sense of the word. It should be a warm and inclusive environment. It should be affirming of each person's uniqueness and individuality. It should be one that celebrates its diversity and recognizes the dignity of *all* people. It should be one where young people feel they are an integral part of the Body of Christ. It should be a Church that calls them to an active discipleship—a discipleship that both nurtures and challenges them to act justly, love tenderly, and walk humbly with their God (see Micah 6:8).

Chapter Questions

1. What is your image of the Church? Is your image multicultural? What might be missing from your image that needs to be included?
2. What kinds of assumptions or biases do you have that might interfere with being truly sensitive and aware of diversity issues? How has your own cultural upbringing influenced your assumptions and biases?
3. Are there characteristics of the dominant culture that you find affirming? nurturing? oppressing? excluding? How might your awareness and identification of those characteristics aid in your work with adolescents?
4. Do you hold a "benevolent tolerance of the others" or a "sincere reverence of others in their otherness"? What steps might you take to move more actively toward achieving a "sincere reverence"?

5. Do you have your own example of a successful program model that promotes the multicultural dimension of youth ministry in a way that empowers youth? What might that example be?

Chapter 15

Catholic Youth Ministry in a School Setting

Michelle Hernandez

Introduction

> Catholic schools create a living faith community in which young people are empowered to utilize their gifts and talents and to live their faith through a variety of meaningful roles in the school, the parish, and in the Church at large. (*Renewing the Vision*, p. 14)

One of the unique dimensions of the Catholic Church's ministry to young people is the extensive school system in many dioceses. Catholic schools provide a unique opportunity for young people to learn about the Gospel of Jesus Christ and to bring the values of the Church into their lives and the world. In addition to religious education, campus ministry and Catholic school communities can foster the faith development of young people through effective religious education and a variety of programs and activities that are designed to make the youth's faith come alive.

Objectives

This chapter applies the goals, themes, and components of comprehensive ministry with adolescents to the Catholic high school setting, describes critical dimensions of school and campus life through a youth ministry lens, and discusses organizational structures and roles in a campus ministry program.

The Vision Reviewed

Catholic schools provide a holistic environment for young people in which the cognitive, affective, and behavioral dimensions of discipleship can be fostered. Through an extensive theology curriculum, students become knowledgeable in Church teachings and traditions, enabling an informed faith to become a lived faith. The theology classroom provides an environment where daily the Church's story is appropriated, where applications and implications in the world are made, and where legitimate questions are valued as integral to the learning process.

In addition to theology, Catholic schools provide ongoing opportunities to deepen students' relationship with Jesus, internalize their understandings of God, and support the process of making faith their own. Retreats, days of reflection, and small faith-sharing or Scripture study groups provide students a particular sense of the relevance their Catholic faith has to their lives. Regular liturgy, seasonal prayer experiences, and daily morning prayer are each avenues for deepening faith.

Catholic schools also provide opportunities for putting faith into action, including students' participation in school liturgies, serving on campus ministry teams, leading campus activities, engaging in service-learning experiences, and bringing students into direct-service and social-justice opportunities. A holistic vision of campus life fosters a comprehensive understanding of discipleship.

A comprehensive understanding of a school's educational mission values students as active participants in their educational experience. Catholic schools are challenged to foster students' active involvement in school activities, religious celebrations, and service opportunities. Integral to that goal is a ministry of welcome and invitation for both students and faculty. Reaching out and involving students and faculty in campus ministry activities, enabling young people to take on leadership roles, and providing necessary leadership and ministry skills are expressions of responsible participation.

A commitment to students' responsible participation requires that a school move beyond the campus or peer ministry team so that participation in campus life is not exclusive to designated peer ministers. Involving the entire student body and the faculty and staff in campus activities more fully creates a school community where the Gospel is lived and experienced and where the entire school community experiences a sense of ownership.

The Catholic school provides a unique setting—through its curriculum, and its extracurricular and school activities—to foster healthy personal and spiritual development in young people. A comprehensive campus ministry provides opportunities for spiritual growth through regular and seasonal prayer and worship experiences, faith-sharing programs, and retreats. Though personal and spiritual growth are integrally related, schools also have a more significant impact on student development by incorporating an intentional approach to asset building (as described in chapter 13 by the Search Institute) into the various dimensions of campus life.

Through mentoring activities, healthy adult-teen relationships, and the modeling of faith-filled adults, the personal and spiritual growth of young people is greatly affected by the faculty and staff. The Catholic school is a significant gift to young people, especially when the mission, programs, and faculty share a commitment to comprehensive education.

Components of a Vision

The three goals of youth ministry are enfleshed in eight components that provide a comprehensive framework through which the dimensions of the school can be integrated into a ministry vision. Though described throughout this text, these components have specific application to campus life:

- *Advocacy.* Providing opportunities for the voice of students in decisions that affect them in the various dimensions of school life.
- *Catechesis.* Providing an intentional and systematic presentation of the Church's teaching, traditions, and rituals, informing and forming students in their faith.
- *Community life.* Creating a sense of connectedness to one another and to the school community as a whole.
- *Evangelization.* Sharing the Good News of Jesus through word and witness by reaching out to those who are not baptized, to the unchurched, to those not raised in the faith, or to those struggling to form their faith.
- *Justice and service.* Integrating the Church's social teachings into the curriculum, instilling compassion, and providing opportunities for students to live out discipleship in service to others.
- *Leadership.* Calling forth the gifts of young people and adults and providing opportunities for them to serve in leadership roles and to carry out the school's vision.
- *Pastoral care.* Fostering healthy adolescent development, assisting young people in times of crisis, and developing a ministry of compassionate presence.

- *Prayer and worship.* Offering a variety of opportunities and settings to worship and pray together as a school community, in small groups, and individually.

Themes for Catholic Youth Ministry

The mission of a school and its youth ministry programs must include the themes presented in *Renewing the Vision.* The following themes are of particular concern in the high school setting.

Family Friendly

Renewing the Vision challenges the faith community to respond to the changing needs of families and to develop strategies to reach out to them. Schools have a particular advantage in reaching out to families, if families are invested in their children's education. Schools can provide regular communication with parents, develop or make available resources for parents, and foster parents' involvement in school activities. Partnering with parents in developing a shared approach to fostering the development of assets in young people would be a significant contribution to the well-being of young people.

Intergenerational

The school campus provides numerous opportunities for young people to build relationships with, share faith with, and learn from adults serving on school faculty and staff. Additionally, schools are challenged to be creative in how parents are involved in extracurricular programs.

Multicultural

Activities, prayers, music, and other campus ministry programs should not only focus on the ethnicity of the student body, but also expose the students to the diverse culture that exists within the

Catholic Church. That can be addressed through the curriculum in the religion department as well as through issues raised in the English, social studies, and foreign language departments, to suggest a few. Schools should also incorporate various ethnic traditions, values, and rituals into their campus ministry programs wherever applicable. Collaborating with a neighboring school, church, or cultural organization is a particularly effective strategy.

Communitywide Collaboration

Forging partnerships with local churches, elementary schools, agencies, and organizations can be an asset to students, to the school, and to the larger community. The service-learning movement is a wonderful avenue for developing such partnerships. Schools are increasingly partnering with community organizations to provide services ranging from Christmas gift programs, home repair, neighborhood cleanups, and visits to the home-bound to tutoring and retreats for elementary school students. Community organizations can also provide interconnectedness between direct and indirect service and advocacy on behalf of those who are in need. Pastoral care is a second significant arena for collaboration. Community organizations and social services can provide resources and staff assistance in the midst of a crisis affecting a school's students. Similarly, such organizations can provide faculty in-services on important issues and training for campus ministry teams.

Leadership

Implementing a holistic vision of ministry with young people in a school setting requires "mobilizing *all* the resources of the faith community in a comprehensive and integrated approach" (*Renewing the Vision*, p. 24). The bishops point out the importance of cooperation among the leaders, ministries, and various programs within the faith community in order to achieve the three goals of youth ministry. If indeed it takes an entire village, someone has to mobilize the village. In a high school setting, the "mobilizer" first and foremost is the administration, along with either the campus ministry coordinator or designates, usually someone from the theology department or another faculty member. This leader must solicit support from and collaboration among administration, faculty, pastor(s), school board, and others while advocating for a shared vision of youth ministry.

Flexible and Adaptable Programs

The school campus serves young people at several developmental stages, and teaching methodologies and activities both within and outside the classroom need to take that into account. Further, even within an academic schedule, a diversity of educational formats, settings, and teaching methodologies should be utilized. Schools are challenged to consider intergenerational programs, small-group experiences, mentoring, and family programs to respond to the changing realities and needs of young people and their families.

Dimensions of Campus Life

Certain essential elements are integral to schools. Those elements of campus life, though, contribute to the unique character of Catholic schools when viewed through the lens of comprehensive youth ministry. The following list includes practical and pastoral applications of a Catholic vision of education.

Mission Statement

The mission statement is the public articulation of the school's purpose for being. It is the starting point for school personnel, as well as for students and their families, the local church community, and the larger community, to share the vision of the Catholic school's role in ministry with young people.

Catholic Identity and Literacy

Fostering Catholic identity is central to a school's mission, and achieving religious literacy is fundamental to that mission. Catholic identity and literacy is enhanced through curriculum and in extracurricular activities, such as small faith or Bible study groups, spiritual direction sessions, retreats, liturgy and prayer, and service. Ministry should encompass all aspects of school life, including crosscurricular faith formation, student government, national honor society, athletics, and so forth. Catholic identity is also reflected in the school's art and environment, especially during special seasons or feasts throughout the year and in promotion and publicity materials. A visitor to the local school should be able to see that the school is Catholic just by walking through the doors. Connecting with the larger Church through diocesan and national youth gatherings also strengthens students' sense of Catholic identity.

Pastoral Care Approach

Pastoral care as a lens for the school environment requires a comprehensive approach to fostering the personal and spiritual growth of young people. A pastoral care approach includes three elements: prevention and promotion strategies for healthy adolescent development; crisis intervention strategies, a crisis intervention plan, and a referral process; and services and resources for families (for example, parenting skills, adult catechesis, literacy skills).

An approach to asset building enhances the pastoral care aspect of youth ministry and can be incorporated into curricular and extracurricular activities. It is also an effective starting point for responding to the parents of students, providing them with an understanding of, and strategies for, fostering the assets in their children.

Prayer Experiences

A critical element in Catholic schools is the opportunity to pray on both communal and personal levels. Daily prayer that is well planned sets a tone and communicates that a school takes prayer seriously. Similarly, liturgies celebrated for the entire student body, for individual classes, or for particular courses can be meaningful experiences for young people. Reconciliation or penance services offer a means of personal prayer and reflection. Various paraliturgical celebrations (during Advent, Lent, Thanksgiving, or times of crisis) can be occasions for both personal and communal prayer. Schools should also take advantage of particular feasts or occasions that add a multicultural dimension to prayer (the tradition of the Saint Joseph Altar, the feast day of Our Lady of Guadalupe, and the feast day of Martin de Porres, for example).

Care should be given to involving students in planning various prayer and worship experiences, and to enabling their participation in liturgical roles. This is also an opportunity to partner students with faculty or staff, fostering relationships outside the classroom.

Justice and Service

The starting point for justice and service activities is to incorporate Catholic social teachings in the curriculum. However, the Church's social ministry can also become the lens of awareness throughout school activities, whether in a service-oriented club, schoolwide drives, or service projects (individual, group, class, or schoolwide).

Justice as an academic experience is greatly enhanced when coupled with service opportunities. Utilizing guest speakers from among the faculty, staff, and parents is an effective methodology for justice education, but it also deepens the network between student, faculty, and parent communities. Involving faculty, staff, and parents in service opportunities, school assemblies, and prayer focusing on justice themes enhances intergenerational relationships. Justice also applies to how the school is run, how funds are allocated, the type and costs of student activities, and how students and faculty are treated by one another and the administration.

Spirit and Spirituality

For young people, a sense of community is reflected in their spirit, their enthusiasm, and their pride in their school. The challenge is to be intentional about creating an atmosphere and environment that says "We are part of something special," where students feel cared for, accepted, and respected. That spirit should certainly be reflected within the school campus, but also when students are off campus at athletic events, trips, service projects, and other school gatherings. Further, that "something special" is deepened by a connection to the larger community, especially through the lens of faith. All students are part of a global Church and the human family. That is the beginning of a justice consciousness.

Connection with the Larger Church

In *Renewing the Vision*, the bishops reiterate Sr. Thea Bowman's adapted phrase, "It takes a whole church[15]" (p. 19). The bishops clearly state that families, parishes, and schools must work together for the Church to achieve the three goals for youth ministry. Neither schools nor students exist in isolation. Both are surrounded by parishes and dioceses that offer connections and resources that can enhance the school ministry experience.

The school should never replace the parish as the primary faith community. It is the task of campus ministry to support and direct students and families to participation in parish life. It is important to connect students with their parish so that they will grow from and contribute to parish life beyond their high school years. Campus ministry coordinators need to encourage students to volunteer within their church, be involved in their parish youth ministry programs, and worship with their parish faith community. In addition, campus leaders should communicate with parish pastoral leaders, especially youth ministers and directors of religious education. Pastors and parish youth-ministry leaders should be invited to visit the school and attend liturgies, assemblies, or other events. Schools need to identify ways to involve the local parishes that contribute to a high school, such as having representation on the school board or parents' clubs from each parish if feasible. Dioceses can also provide a wealth of resources for schools. Guest speakers, videos, and print resources may be helpful for the theology classes or for larger assemblies. Dioceses also provide training programs for youth and adults, retreats, service projects, pilgrimages, youth gatherings, and connections to national youth gatherings. Minimally, schools should foster their connections with the diocesan school, religious-education, youth-ministry, and social-justice offices.

Faculty and Staff as Ministers

Schools with a Catholic vision enable the faculty and staff to see their work and their role as ministry. The school provides faculty and staff with retreats or days of reflection, prayer experiences, and community-building opportunities. When viewed through the ministry lens, the role of teacher extends beyond classroom and curriculum. Teaching becomes a vocation, and the faculty become active participants in fostering the assets and faith life of young people, and education becomes a mutual activity in which the teacher is open to learning from the experiences of young people. Such a faculty and staff participate in the wide range of campus ministry activities provided for the students, valuing the opportunities for building relationships with students.

Administration

The administrators of the Catholic school are the faith leaders of the school community. The administration sets the tone of a school. When taken seriously, a Catholic vision of education impacts the role of the administration, the policies and procedures that govern both students and faculty, and the accessibility of the administration to students, parents, and faculty. The administration must be a pastoral presence in a youth-friendly environment. Recognizing their investment and participation in the school community, students and faculty should be involved in decision making where appropriate. School policies regarding pregnancy, violence, drug and alcohol use, or other disciplinary issues should reflect both a pastoral understanding and prudent procedures.

Academic Excellence and Life Skills

Schools must prepare their students to live and lead in the twenty-first century with a solid base of Christian values. To take seriously the goal of fostering personal and spiritual growth requires that in addition to the basic academic skills, students need life skills such as skills for critical thinking, decision making, problem solving, conflict management, relationship building, and faith, including prayer and worship, the use of the Scriptures, discernment, moral decision making, and the application of Catholic social teaching to national and international events. Those skills can be taught through the curriculum, clubs and activities, assemblies, and other avenues that are available through the school.

Conclusion

Indeed, it takes an entire village to raise a child and to foster faith in young people. Catholic youth ministry provides the Church village with a comprehensive approach that can be fully integrated into a school setting. However, that requires a vision, a structure, a coordinator, and the commitment of the entire school community. To do so, though, is to create "something special."

Chapter Questions

1. What are some ways parents, faculty, and staff can be more involved in a Catholic school's existing programs?
2. What is one strategy a school can implement to strengthen families or empower parents?
3. How might a Catholic high school foster the multicultural dimension of ministry with its young people?
4. What are some ways the local Catholic high school could reach out to local parishes and to diocesan offices? What strategies might parishes consider for reaching out to the local Catholic high school?
5. Consider a local Catholic high school. How must the campus ministry program be adapted in order to become more comprehensive? What are the current strengths? the current challenges?
6. Analyze and rewrite the local Catholic high school's mission statement to include a comprehensive approach to and vision of youth ministry.

Chapter 16

Organizing for Catholic Youth Ministry

Sean Reynolds

Introduction

In organizing youth ministry, three principal interlocking tasks need to be launched and coordinated: planning, developing appropriate structures to carry out the plans, and managing a leadership development system to raise up leaders, youth and adults, who will inhabit the structures and fulfill the plans. Those three tasks can be daunting for the novice, and even experienced youth ministry leaders struggle to maintain the rhythm. Happily, the objective isn't perfection. Rather, the objective is to develop an ongoing system of planning, organization, and discipleship that will sustain fruitful youth ministry.

Objectives

This chapter provides the basics for planning comprehensive youth ministry programs by delineating a detailed planning process, describing the necessary organizational structures for youth ministry, explaining basic principles of organizational development, and outlining a leadership development system.

Planning Effective Youth Ministry

What is needed is a planning process that brings the needs of young people together with the vision described in *Renewing the Vision* in developing an overall strategy that advances the goals of comprehensive youth ministry in a given faith community.

Assessing Needs

It is vital for youth ministry to be shaped by the unique needs of the individual faith community. Whether by means of interviews, questionnaires, focus groups, census research, demographic analysis, or other means, the planning process must be informed by trustworthy information about the needs of young people, which will guide subsequent decisions.

Developing Vision and Mission

Youth ministry planners need a compelling vision and a clear sense of mission as a framework from within which to respond to needs. *Renewing the Vision* serves mightily in simplifying that step for youth ministry leaders, as it can provide much of the framework and language. Parish or school vision and mission statements, if extant, should also be used as foundational resources for the development of statements of youth ministry vision and mission, because the vision and mission of a faith community's youth ministry ideally will flow from the vision and mission of that faith community.

Setting Goals and Objectives

This step engages planners in naming the hoped-for outcomes of their efforts. Without goals and objectives, the evaluation step is frequently limited to how well participants liked or didn't like a particular program—helpful information, but if that's all there is, we have little sense of how well our efforts are effectively realizing our vision and mission, or responding to identified needs.

Developing a Calendar of Programs, Activities, and Events

Youth ministry planners frequently will skip the preceding planning steps and begin their planning process here, which is understandable: good-willed people with limited time want to get right down to the business of serving young people. Unfortunately, if that step is not informed by the previous ones, the whims of the planners rather than the mission of the Church will almost certainly guide the planning.

This step is perhaps the most creative, as planners brainstorm, prioritize, and make decisions on the variety of programs, strategies, activities, and events that will fill the youth ministry calendar. These are some important considerations for planners at this point in the process:

- *Schedule modestly and realistically.* Keep in mind that "things always take longer than they take."
- *Compare calendars.* With the pace of life today, there's no way to completely avoid schedule conflicts. They can, however, be minimized by checking and cross-checking parish, school, and community calendars.

- *Use the liturgical year as the planning template.* Utilize the established framework of the movements and feasts of the liturgical year as the basis of the youth ministry calendar. That means not only avoiding conflicts with parish opportunities for worship, service, education, and celebration, but in fact featuring those opportunities prominently on the youth ministry calendar.
- *Plan across the components.* Strive for balance among the components, with emphasis on those identified as high priority in the needs-assessment step.
- *Keep in mind gathered v. nongathered approaches.* Resist the temptation to over-program gathered approaches to the exclusion of nongathered ones.
- *Keep in mind the full range of ministry settings.* Remember that the family, the parish, the school, and the civic community are all potential arenas for ministry.

Implementing the Calendar

This is one of the principal points of intersection with the youth ministry structure and leadership development system. Once the planners map out the calendar, people need to be organized and delegate the responsibility for implementing it. Leaders of many kinds—catechists, chaperones, presenters, cooks, drivers, and so on—need to be recruited, oriented, trained, empowered, supported, and managed, in the context of an organizational framework that might contain committees, task groups, teams, boards, and commissions.

Evaluation

Programs, projects, strategies, activities, and events should ideally be evaluated at their conclusion, or soon thereafter. Participant evaluations are invaluable in that regard, whether in questionnaire form or otherwise. However, the results of such evaluations are only one part of the evaluation task. The further and more important task of evaluation is to assess how well those programs, projects, strategies, activities, and events impacted goals and objectives, and in so doing, furthered the vision and mission. The planning group should periodically review the statements of vision and mission, as well as the goals and objectives, to determine how well they are being achieved.

Evaluation results are then fed back into the ongoing youth ministry planning and calendaring. Programming and strategies that successfully contribute to the vision, mission, goals, and objectives are maintained and developed. Programming that is found significantly wanting should be either dramatically revised or discontinued.

The Planning Cycle

Planning is not a once-and-for-all-time affair. The latter steps of the process (developing a calendar of programs, and so on) take place on a regular cycle that works best for the planners and faith community, sometimes on a quarterly, semiannual, or annual basis. The early steps in the process (formal needs assessment, revising vision and mission statements, setting goals and objectives) happen less frequently. Needs, vision, and mission will likely need serious review and revision every few years. Goals and objectives typically demand at least annual review, and may require anything from fine-tuning to a complete overhaul, depending on evaluation results.

Developing Effective Youth Ministry Structures

In the Beginning . . . The Evolution of Youth Ministry

In the beginning there was the parish youth club. One or a few adult leaders would gather with parish youth in weekly or biweekly meetings, mainly to hang out and plan social events or athletic outings. Usually young people were elected as officers. The adults served mainly as advisers and moderators. Catechetical and spiritual content was typically minimal. There may have been a few service opportunities in the mix, but it was mainly a Church social club for young people. The calendar contained hayrides, dances, canoeing, holiday parties, and baseball games, with regular meetings to hold it all together. God smiled and saw that it was good.

Then came the youth group. Elections were left behind because the leaders realized that they became popularity contests and were counterproductive to the sense of community they were trying to build. Adult leaders planned the meetings, assisted by some "leadership youth." In their wisdom the leaders understood that CCD and school religion classes weren't enough, so they began to add more catechetical and spiritual content, and maybe more service; prayer services, retreats, leaf raking, a road trip or two to a youth conference or mission-service site began to appear on the Church calendar. God smiled and saw that these new things were very good indeed.

But then the adult leaders began to murmur among themselves, saying, "We always seem to get the same kids, and our numbers never seem to grow beyond a certain point." The murmuring increased as their diocesan leaders shared about something called "total youth ministry." The adult leaders were dismayed: How could they accomplish all that with their humble youth group? God smiled and saw that the dismay was good.

And the adult leaders said to one another: "Alas, a youth group alone cannot sustain all those goals and components. What shall we do?" Like an answer to heartfelt prayer, the core team was born. A core team brought more leaders, both youth and adults, into the planning process, and more was accomplished, much more—and more youth were added to their number. God smiled, approved, and saw that these developments were good, very good indeed.

Yet the leaders began again to chafe and murmur: the vision of youth ministry and this new core team approach opened up endless possibilities, but they seemed blocked and bounded by the youth group, which continued as the principal format of youth ministry. Although larger in number, the group still engaged only a fraction of the total number of youth in the parish. The core team found itself planning a breadth of wonderful ministry opportunities for a limited number of people: the youth group. Then, in a flash of insight, the leaders declared, "Let us minister not only to the youth group but to youth groupings, according to their needs and interests!"

Only with great difficulty did they painstakingly begin to pry their thinking and ministry loose from the youth-group model. But as they did, marvelous things began to happen as the ministry swelled to include many different groupings of youth. Those who were utterly uninterested in a regular youth-group meeting began to attend Bible studies or served with Habitat for Humanity or joined the choir. Once the leaders began to "think outside the box" of youth group, youth ministry exploded. And God saw this, smiled broadly, and said, "Outstanding!"

And so it came to pass that the core team evolved into program and project teams, each responsible for a different aspect of youth ministry. Young people got involved as they were interested and able. Youth ministry programming reflected the full spectrum of components. A single youth group was gradually replaced by youth and adults joining forces in many different kinds of groupings, pursuing a rich variety of ministry needs and aims. God smiled indeed, but God wasn't finished yet!

Then the youth ministry leaders began to murmur among themselves about feeling utterly overwhelmed; the new approach was crushing them with multiple meetings, programs, projects, task forces, and committees. They complained of becoming administrators rather than ministers, and felt they were losing touch with their mission. They struggled with the complexity of multiple teams and flow charts and scheduling nightmares. The wisest among them asked themselves: "What have we wrought? Why are we wearing ourselves out trying to build a separate church for young people alongside the rest of the faith community? Why are we trying to replicate in our youth ministry programming the life that is available for everyone else in the faith community?"

Of course and as usual, God heard their supplications, and God said (through the publication of *Renewing the Vision*): "Let the faith community thrive and multiply and be abundant with youth! Let the young people take their place at the table, and let them not be separated as chaff from wheat! Let them, in their full dignity as baptized and fully initiated members of their faith communities, participate side by side with everyone else in the life and ministries of the faith community!"

And so it was (with great and utter relief!) that youth ministry leaders realized they did not have to create special youth projects and programs for all the components out on the margins of the faith community, but that their planning and programming needed to lead young people back into the heart of the parish. Rather than having to provide a full menu of prayer, catechetical, social, or service events exclusively for youth, they could clear the way for youth to be involved in the prayer, catechesis, social, and service events *of the faith community!*

And so it is today. And God smiles and sees that it is indeed very, very good.

Principles of Organizational Development

As noted in the preceding section, the unfolding experience of contemporary Catholic youth ministry necessitated a rethinking and redesign of the organizational formats necessary to carry the vision forward. Obviously and sometimes painfully, this dynamic process of development also entails letting go of organizational structures that are no longer capable of carrying the vision.

Over time, healthy organizations will cycle through stages of appraisal and reorganization so as to develop new structures that might more effectively carry the vision, and to let go of structures that no longer fit the reality of the current needs and mission. Ideally, the pace of the cycle will accommodate the tolerance of participants for change: too-frequent changes can result in chaos, and too little change can lead to stagnation. Part of the art of effective leadership is to monitor and facilitate the appropriate pace of change. Effective youth ministry leadership needs to understand the dynamics of structural organizational change; it must be capable of initiating the development of new structures as needed and helping people let go of structures that no longer fit current and future needs. In this, youth ministry leaders act as architects and therapists: on the one hand, providing blueprints for change and directing the building or rebuilding process; and on the other hand, facilitating a grieving process as people learn to let go of outdated organizational structures.

The Youth Ministry Leader as Architect

Youth ministry leaders need to understand the "master blueprint" for youth ministry described in *Renewing the Vision*. The "function" of youth ministry structures is ultimately to accomplish the three goals of youth ministry and to sustain the components of youth ministry in an ongoing way in a faith community. To make that vision a reality, youth ministry leaders need to understand the building blocks of youth ministry organizations and how those building blocks fit together. Finally, youth ministry leaders need to be able to orchestrate the building process.

The Master Blueprint

In preceding chapters, *Renewing the Vision* was explored in detail. The three goals of *Renewing the Vision* are the three cornerstones of any youth ministry building project. Ultimately, any structures that are devised should be at the service of one or more of the three goals of youth ministry. Conversely, structures that do not seem to serve one or more of the goals should be carefully scrutinized, using the following questions, and if found to be lacking, discarded:

- *Goal 1.* Does this structure positively impact the ability of young people to follow Christ, to live the Gospel, and to participate in the transformation of society?
- *Goal 2.* Does this structure assist young people in becoming fully participating members of the faith community?
- *Goal 3.* Does this structure positively impact the healthy development of adolescents—spiritually, socially, physically, emotionally, and psychologically?

These goals, alone or in combination, are the "acid test" of the usefulness of particular youth ministry structures. Ideally, structures will positively impact all the goals. Structures that have little or no impact on realizing the goals should be let go.

Organizational Building Blocks

As architects of youth ministry structure, what are the fundamental building blocks at our disposal? Too frequently the typical default response to that question is limited to "youth group." In many of our Catholic parishes, that is virtually the only youth ministry structure under consideration, even though it is dated and inherently unable to sustain the vision and components of youth ministry. Although it is for many parishes the initial building block of their youth ministry, it is woefully inadequate.

> The problem, we have discovered after a hundred years of youth groups, is that the youth group is notoriously unreliable for fostering ongoing *faith*. The youth group model—some-

times referred to as the "one-eared Mickey Mouse" model of ministry—created an environment in which youth, isolated in an "ear" on top of Mickey's head, had only marginal contact with the body of Christ. (Kenda Creasy Dean and Ron Foster, *The Godbearing Life,* p. 30)

Youth ministry leaders in their role as architects of youth ministry structure need a repertoire of organizational building blocks with which to assemble a structure that works for a parish.

If You Build It, They Will Come

As an architect of youth ministry organizational structures, a director or coordinator of youth ministry needs to both manage the current youth ministry organization, such as it is, and develop and launch new structures to meet emerging ministry needs and goals. Using the various commissions and teams noted previously as generic building blocks, youth ministry leaders have at their disposal powerful tools for discipleship and the empowerment of individuals and groups who will take responsibility for different aspects of youth ministry.

That leads us to the third of the three principals noted at the beginning of this chapter—and perhaps the most challenging one of all: building a leadership development system that effectively multiplies the heads, hearts, and hands available to make ministry happen.

Building the Leadership Development System

As an architect of youth ministry structure, a director or coordinator of youth ministry quickly needs to turn attention to populating that structure with people who will take responsibility for leading or contributing to its many different tasks and responsibilities. That involves much more than simply finding volunteers. It means integrating into the overall structure an ongoing system that locates, recruits, prepares, manages, and nurtures volunteer leaders and helpers. Depending on the complexity and sophistication of the youth ministry structure, such a system can itself be fairly simple or quite complex.

Preparation

Before beginning to call others into partnership in ministry, the youth ministry leader should create a flow chart, schematic, or diagram that visually captures the way people will be organized and will interact, collaborate, and communicate with one another. Then, based on that diagram, the task is to identify the specific roles and numbers and kinds of people who will be needed to make the structures work.

Prayer is the other vital part of preparation: prayer that God's living Spirit will stir the hearts of those who may be called to join the ministry. In the complicated process of organizing a youth ministry structure, it is not difficult to lose sight of the essential spiritual underpinnings of our efforts. Prayer keeps our sights fixed on the nonnegotiable foundation of all ministry: our relationship of utter dependence on God. It is God's Spirit who draws hearts to ministry, and our prayer acknowledges our reliance on God to bring forth workers for the vineyard.

Developing Job Descriptions and Profiles

As a general rule, the more clearly and specifically a task or responsibility is defined, the more likely it is an individual will agree to take it on. No one appreciates receiving an ill-defined task. For that reason it is important to do the preliminary work of developing job descriptions for the roles identified in the structural blueprint. A job description clearly defines and sets limits to the tasks, areas of responsibility, length of term, lines of accountability, level of authority, and so on. Having those matters clarified at the front end can obviate serious misunderstandings later on.

Based on the job description, a profile may be developed that details the particular qualities of the person being sought. A profile assists recruiters in seeking people with the specific strengths and capabilities suited to a particular role.

Recruiting

Fortified with prayer and armed with a structural blueprint, job descriptions, and profiles, youth ministry leaders are well prepared to begin recruiting. Some general suggestions for effective recruiting include these:

- Explore various high potential sources, including recent RCIA participants, young-adult groups, graduates returning from college, parents of teenagers, teachers, coaches, new parish members, and so on. The pastor and staff members, even the parish secretary, can be rich sources of information on potential recruits, as can parish census data.
- Use the parish bulletin, announcements, and stewardship events to get the word out, but don't expect written advertisements to be more than minimally effective. Few people get involved by responding to public notices; most are drawn in because of direct, personal invitation.
- Use profiles and job descriptions to recruit individuals for specific roles according to their capabilities, gifts, and strengths. Seek them out individually and personally. Affirm their gifts. Be enthusiastic, and be sure not to under-represent the level and length of commitment involved. People respond well to a challenge and they appreciate honesty; they run from any scent of manipulation or dishonesty.
- In a gesture appropriate to the level of commitment involved, seal the arrangement with as little as a handshake or as much as a public commissioning service.

Orientation, Training, Team Building

Once people are recruited and their commitment secured, they will need guidance and support of different kinds, commensurate with their roles. Orientation provides an opportunity for further clarification of roles and responsibilities, specific information necessary to get started, and the opportunity to begin relationships with others who will be serving. Training provides more in-depth development of the knowledge and capabilities necessary to effectively fill roles. Team-building activities further develop relationships and effectiveness by enhancing communication, cooperation, and collaboration.

Supporting, Nurturing, Managing, and Leading

Recruits typically require different levels and kinds of support from ministry leaders. Some need a great deal of initial support and hand-holding; others much less. That is part of the fine art of ministry leadership: the ability to assess the particular needs of individual recruits and to provide the most helpful support. Youth ministry leaders should provide for ongoing evaluation, training, group building, and spiritual and emotional support as needed and desired by volunteers. The volunteer experience should be regularly seasoned with expressions of gratitude and praise. Effective management, including attention to detail in scheduling, communication, delegation, and follow-through on promised resources, is critical to the health and well-being of volunteer ministers. Moreover, youth ministry leaders who both "walk the talk and talk the walk" provide the kind of inspirational, motivational leadership that others need to stay focused on their service with commitment and a smile.

Evaluating and Celebrating

Youth ministry leaders are responsible for periodic, ongoing evaluation of volunteer ministers. Ideally, this will take place by prior arrangement, so it won't be a surprise to volunteers. The opportunity for feedback and dialogue about roles, tasks, and responsibilities, as well as the chance to engage in problem solving around particular issue areas, can serve as a tremendous support to volunteers. In that way volunteers are also welcomed into an ongoing process of self-development in the ministry, which serves to keep the experience fresh and healthy.

The volunteer experience should ideally be punctuated with frequent expressions and celebrations of gratitude, honoring the generosity of individuals' contributions and the fine ministry efforts accomplished. Volunteer service warrants special notice and celebration at the conclusion of a person's terms of service.

Volunteers should also be included in evaluation of the mission, goals, and programs of the youth ministry effort. They possess firsthand information about successes, failures, challenges, and graces—information invaluable to the ongoing processes of planning and implementation.

Ongoing Preparation, Fine-Tuning, and Development

Leadership development is an ongoing mission and challenge of the youth ministry effort, intimately linked to *Renewing the Vision's* first goal of discipleship. It's always a work in progress, and is never ultimately finished. As such, an effective leadership development system is integrated into the fabric of youth ministry as part of the ministry's infrastructure: there will always be a need for more leaders and volunteers, filling new roles generated out of emerging ministry needs and priorities and replacing those who move on.

In that sense the work of leadership development is cyclical, and inevitably endings lead back to beginnings. Prayer for new volunteers is ongoing. Fine-tuning job descriptions and profiles proceeds as needed. Volunteers are recruited throughout the year, but especially in accord with needs predicted by the planning process and youth ministry calendar. Because of the ongoing nature of the leadership development tasks, it can be enormously helpful to include a leadership development team on the master youth ministry structural blueprint. Such a team might relieve the burden from the director or coordinator of youth ministry of ongoing recruiting and cultivation of new volunteers, simultaneously infusing new life and vitality into the ministry.

Chapter Questions

1. Describe the current leadership structure for your parish's youth ministry effort.
2. What are the strengths and weaknesses relative to the threefold tasks of planning, building structure, and developing leadership in your parish community? How might the parish further develop the strengths and address the weaknesses?
3. What changes in planning, structure, and leadership development might yield the greatest fruit in your faith community's youth ministry?
4. Choose a particular function in youth ministry (program leader, retreat director, service coordinator, and so on) and create a detailed job description for that position.

Chapter 17

Leadership for Catholic Youth Ministry

Sean Reynolds

Introduction

Clearly there is no easy predictor of success and effectiveness in youth ministry (evidenced by the vast and sobering number of energetic young adults who have been hired as youth ministers, only to fail, be fired, fade away, or move to more lucrative careers). Effective youth ministry leadership defies easy, offhand explanation. Yet understand it we must if we are to recruit, develop, nurture, and sustain leadership equipped to build comprehensive youth ministry.

Objectives

This chapter describes the basic characteristics of youth ministry leadership, outlines the changing understanding of the role of the youth ministry leader, and introduces the *National Certification Standards for Lay Ecclesial Ministers.*

Youth Ministry Leadership: Common Threads

Some clear commonalities exist among those who excel in youth ministry. Present to a greater or lesser degree, those common characteristics seem to propel youth ministry leaders through challenges and obstacles that turn others aside from the ministry.

Vibrant, Lived Faith

Effective youth ministry leaders are truly excited about living out God's call. They are convincing because they don't need to be convinced of the intrinsic value of integral, lived faith. They have credibility because their "walk matches their talk." There is no one pattern for how that faith is lived—or even the precise content of that faith—yet lived, owned faith is a constant among them. They are passionate about life with and in God, and that passion buoys them in turbulent times and grounds them in the face of adversity. They express that faith in countless ways: from Eucharistic adoration to inner-city service, from daily Mass to spiritual direction, from praying the rosary to centering prayer. Yet the common thread is a passionate commitment to God, in Christ, through the Holy Spirit.

Commitment to Ongoing Education and Formation

Without exception, youth ministers who remain in the ministry for any length of time manifest a commitment to personal and professional development. Either through formal degree programs or a history of scattered continuing education opportunities, effective youth ministry leaders find ways to learn how to grow more effective. They are frequent attendees at workshops, seminars, conferences, symposia, courses, spiritual direction sessions, in-services, retreats, lectures, and so on. They thirst for more knowledge, enhanced skills, and deepened faith.

Meaningful Connection with a Faith Community

Effective youth ministry leaders intentionally seek and find ways to be connected with the faith community. That faith community may or may not be the one in which they exercise their leadership; however, it appears to be a nonnegotiable aspect of their vitality, a way of being tapped into a social situation that keeps them grounded, real, whole, praying, and open to the Holy Spirit. It variously calls them to balance—away from overwork into healthier relationships all around. It is a place where they can be real, let their hair down, be themselves, and step out of their role for a while. Effective youth ministry leaders are involved in small faith communities, prayer groups, ministry associations, support groups, pastoral supervision groups, educational communities, and the like.

Team Approach to Ministry

Even the most talented and charismatic leader finds that after a time, leadership can be a lonely and burdensome business. Conversely, the vision of youth ministry described in *Renewing the Vision* is much too broad and comprehensive to be the work of one person. Effective youth ministry leaders, either by personal inclination, ministerial vision, or bone-weariness, find ways to invite others into sharing the ministry. They are team players, not lone rangers. They multiply their ministry by welcoming others into it, training, nurturing, supporting, celebrating, and even sometimes firing them. In that sense they serve not just as youth ministers but as coordinators of youth ministry, orchestrating the efforts of others.

Communicating Vision and Valued Outcomes

Effective youth ministry leaders are able to articulate their vision of youth ministry to make a compelling case for devoting limited time, energies, and resources to youth ministry. They "begin with the end in mind" in their planning and organization of youth ministry, and keep valued goals and outcomes clearly in front of all. They design and offer programs, but they are keenly aware that the programs are not the end but the means to greater goals. The U.S. bishops' vision described in *Renewing the Vision* provides the framework and foundation for those goals and valued outcomes, which make application of that vision to a particular place and time.

Effective Management and Administration

Many a youth ministry program has crashed on the shoals of poor communication, ineffective planning, and inattention to detail. Conversely, careful planning and attention to detail can result in wondrous outcomes. Although often maligned as boring or even nonministerial, administration can truly be a form of servant leadership: not much fun, but vital to the youth ministry project. Advance planning, calendars, schedules, permission forms, flyers, timely communications, budgets, accounting, time management—

all these are nonnegotiable for youth ministry leaders, and if handled well, contribute to the well-being of people and the overall program. Handled poorly, they can translate into dissatisfaction, disappointment, and discouragement, which drain the positive energy from an otherwise vibrant youth ministry effort.

A Historical Snapshot: The Evolution of Catholic Youth Ministry Leadership

The Catholic faith community in the United States has had three distinct phases or movements of youth ministry leadership. The movements correspond directly to the prevalent thinking of each period about what youth ministry is and how to go about it. Understanding those three movements can provide insight into the nature of Catholic youth ministry leadership and can be instructive as to the vital tasks of youth ministry leadership.

Movement One: The Youth Minister

Even prior to the publication of the original guiding Catholic youth ministry document, *A Vision of Youth Ministry,* some visionary parishes had hired youth ministers. They were true pioneers. By and large they had no job descriptions and no clear guidance from pastors or other parish leaders. They were hired to "take care of the parish's youth." Both before and immediately after the publication of that original vision document, youth ministers typically were paid little for working extraordinarily long hours, and were basically inventing Catholic youth ministry on the fly.

The principal format or approach to youth ministry was the youth group, and the youth minister's job was to lead the youth group. In fact, *youth group* and *youth ministry* were substantially identical terms and were used interchangeably. Other forms of a parish's relationship with young people, like religion classes or athletics, were not widely understood to be youth ministry. Youth ministry took place in the youth group, and it was the youth minister who made it happen.

As the principal and often sole youth ministry leader, the youth minister did it all: leading meetings, providing retreats, leading prayer, counseling teenagers, and so forth. In short, the youth minister was understood to be the provider of youth ministry, the single-handed "ministry delivery system," if you will. The conventional lineup of mainstay youth ministry activities was at that time brand new and cutting edge to Catholic settings: icebreakers, group games, creative prayer services, simulation activities, active learning, and so on. In the best of circumstances, the youth minister developed and became adept at a wide array of ministry programs, projects, and techniques.

In the worst of circumstances, the youth minister functioned as something of a "youth guru." In some parishes youth ministry became a cult of personality as the youth minister commanded an unhealthy and slavish followership among youth. As the principal gatekeepers of nearly everything youth oriented in the parish, youth ministers could block initiatives that didn't originate with them. Frequently even the best-intentioned youth ministers simply burned out from the stress and overwork related to a solo approach to ministry.

Movement Two:
The Youth Ministry Coordinator

By the late 1970s, the "youth minister as solo ministry delivery system" was showing serious strain, both as a practical matter and as an effective means of carrying forward the vision of youth ministry. Youth ministers complained, often bitterly, of being overworked and underpaid. Moreover, the goals and components of youth ministry as described in *A Vision of Youth Ministry* were not well-served by this approach because there was no possible way for one person to single-handedly deliver on the promise of such a broad and inclusive vision.

Enter the notion of the youth ministry leader as youth ministry coordinator. National training organizations and diocesan leaders began to assist youth ministers in understanding themselves to be coordinators of ministry. As coordinators of ministry they would be responsible not so much for providing the ministry themselves, but for orchestrating the ministry in concert with others. The role of the youth ministry leader was radically reshaped as a result, and another layer of challenge and responsibility was added to the role.

In addition to providing the ministry themselves, youth ministry leaders began to enlist the support of others, orienting and training them; organizing them; supporting, evaluating, and celebrating them. As ministry coordinators, youth ministers became not only volunteer managers but also, in a sense, entrepreneurs of youth ministry: identifying ministry needs, then orchestrating the people and resources to respond to those needs. This transformation demanded that youth ministers become experts not only at the ministry itself but also at giving away the ministry to others, and at managing the whole affair with different teams, programs, and projects in various stages of planning and implementation.

This development was initially heralded as a practical way for youth ministers to extricate themselves from lone-ranger status and lauded as a way to address the problem of burnout among youth ministers. However, in effect it added much more work, not to mention the daunting task of learning the relevant skills and tools of organizational development and volunteer management. Through the 1980s and beyond, in their role as coordinators, youth ministry leaders learned to meet the dual challenge of providing ministry themselves and of developing a youth ministry infrastructure that would sustain and perpetuate the ministry in their absence. Volunteer partners, youth and adults, were brought into roles on core teams, project or program teams, youth ministry commissions, boards, and the like. Not only were the youth ministers responsible for populating those structures with people, in many cases they were responsible for inventing the structures themselves, drawing up job descriptions, conducting planning sessions to get them moving, and building new structures as needed. The complexity of the role of youth minister expanded exponentially.

Movement Three: The Youth Minister as Animator

In the years leading up to the 1997 publication of *Renewing the Vision,* a third movement organically unfolded. The initial promise of the coordinator role led to mixed results. In parishes with ample resources and capable, visionary leadership, the approach took off.

Youth ministry coordinators recruited volunteers and organized them into core teams, project teams, commissions, and the like. The opportunities available to young people multiplied as more people were invited into and took responsibility for discrete areas of youth ministry.

In parishes with fewer resources or less capable leadership, the approach frequently struggled, limped along, or failed. The complexity involved in developing and orchestrating comprehensive youth ministry could be overwhelming and discouraging, especially for new and inexperienced youth ministry leaders.

Renewing the Vision stirred a radically different approach to youth ministry into the mix. Substantiated by research findings of the Search Institute and others, this was the U.S. bishop's vision:

> Today, we propose a framework for integrating the Church's ministry with adolescents that incorporates a broader, expanded, and more comprehensive vision. First articulated in *A Vision of Youth Ministry* and developed more fully over the past two decades, the comprehensive approach is a framework for integration rather than a specific model. The comprehensive approach is not a single program or recipe for ministry. Rather, it provides a way for integrating ministry with adolescents and their families into the total life and mission of the Church, recognizing that the whole community is responsible for this ministry. (P. 19)

Thus, in this framework youth ministry is neither the work of one person (the youth minister) nor the work of a group of people (the coordinator and volunteers), but is rightly the responsibility of the entire faith community. So evolved the notion of the youth minister as *animator* of the youth ministry of the faith community. The implications of this new paradigm of youth ministry leadership are far reaching and are yet being explored and understood.

If the faith community is, in fact, the youth ministry delivery system, the role of youth ministry leader becomes principally one of helping the faith community and its members wake up to that reality, own it, and actualize it. Instead of the usual pattern of organizing special "youth only" ministry opportunities, the youth minister works to ensure that young people are included in the array of ministry opportunities that already exist in the parish. The youth ministry leader accomplishes that primarily through education, consciousness-raising, and advocacy for youth involvement in the regular day-to-day life of the faith community.

For example, as animator the youth ministry leader advocates for youth involvement in the liturgical and worship life of the faith community. As a practical matter, that might involve conversations with the pastor, worship commission, liturgy coordinator, music minister, choir, and so forth, so as to pave the way for youth involvement. It could mean working behind the scenes to ensure that the usual ways people are recruited and trained for liturgical ministry roles are youth-friendly, hospitable, welcoming, and developmentally appropriate for youth. It could mean convincing the music minister to expand her or his repertoire and instrumentation to include a broader range of musical styles that would be helpful for young worshipers.

In this approach the onus of either providing the ministry oneself (the "youth minister" model), or developing an array of youth ministry opportunities led by teams of volunteers (the "youth ministry coordinator" model) is replaced by the very different challenge of assisting the parish in becoming the *de facto* youth minister.

Youth Ministry Leadership

All three movements of youth ministry leadership are variously represented in our parishes and faith communities today. Youth ministry leaders typically operate out of one, two, or all three approaches, according to their own strengths and inclinations and in response to the needs and resources of the faith community. Experience has shown that all three approaches have their merits. Yet experience has also shown that the "youth minister" and "youth ministry coordinator" approaches are insufficient in responding to the mandate of *Renewing the Vision* to integrate young people into the fabric of the faith community. (Ironically, both the "youth minister" and "youth ministry coordinator" models can actually have the unintended result of leading young people away from deeper involvement in the faith community by providing alternative ministries on or outside the boundaries of parish life—alternatives that can be more attractive because they are exclusively peer-oriented, and as such designed to appeal directly and solely to youth.)

Moreover, youth ministry leaders ideally will be able to function effectively out of all three approaches as needed. Circumstances will variously demand that youth ministry leaders provide the ministry directly and personally, organize others to provide the ministry, and animate the ministry of the faith community on behalf of young people. For instance, youth ministry leaders who devote most of their time and energy toward direct ministry with young people will have little time left for developing a youth ministry infrastructure (goals, administration, development, evaluation, and so forth) or to work to animate the faith community—typically a prescription for burnout. Youth ministry leaders who devote themselves solely to their coordinator role may find themselves functioning exclusively as administrators rather than ministers. Those who emphasize animation to the exclusion of the other approaches will experience the absence of events, activities, and opportunities designed explicitly for youth.

National Certification Standards

A landmark development in the self-understanding of youth ministry leadership took place in 2003 with the publication of *National Certification Standards for Lay Ecclesial Ministers* by three national ministry associations: the National Association for Lay Ministry, the National Conference for Catechetical Leadership, and the National Federation for Catholic Youth Ministry. For several years prior to that publication, representatives of those organizations met and struggled together to identify the core competencies common to the roles of pastoral minister, catechetical leader, and youth ministry leader. From literally hundreds of competency statements, they crystallized the following five core standards:

- *Personal and spiritual maturity.* A lay ecclesial minister demonstrates personal and spiritual maturity in ministry with the people of God.

- *Lay ecclesial ministry identity.* A lay ecclesial minister identifies the call to formal and public ministry as a vocation rooted in Baptism.
- *Catholic theology.* A lay ecclesial minister integrates knowledge of the Catholic faith into ministry.
- *Pastoral praxis.* A lay ecclesial minister engages in pastoral activity that promotes evangelization, faith formation, community, and pastoral care with sensitivity to diverse situations.
- *Professional practice.* A lay ecclesial minister provides effective leadership, administration, and service, in the spirit of collaboration.

(Adapted from pp. 1–11)

Contained in the section on pastoral praxis are specialized standards that describe the competencies relating directly to youth ministry leaders. Taken together, the common and specialized standards paint a portrait of a well-rounded, professionally prepared youth ministry leader with these characteristics:

- exhibits personal maturity through a balanced lifestyle, a positive self-image, and appropriate relationships (p. 1)
- develops a spiritual maturity formed in theological reflection, based on Gospel values, and nurtured in private, communal, and liturgical prayer (p. 1)
- accepts ministerial vocation as a baptismal call from Christ (p. 2)
- articulates and interprets a Catholic understanding of Scripture, tradition, and doctrine, and uses this knowledge to form a community of disciples engaged in the mission of the church (p. 3)
- applies the process of pastoral praxis in building a community of disciples engaged in the transformation of society (p. 7)
- incorporates the dimensions of evangelization, faith formation, worship, inculturation, community, justice, and service within pastoral activities (p. 7)
- understands leadership theory and applies it in a ministerial setting (p. 11)

- demonstrates a knowledge of and ability to work with parish and (arch)diocesan systems and structures (p. 11)
- lives by the code of ethics applicable to ministry and abides by civil and church law (p. 11)

National Certification Standards for Lay Ecclesial Ministers not only provides a comprehensive, in-depth description of the competencies of full-time, staff-level youth ministry leaders, it also may be used, with a bit of adaptation, as a self-assessment tool. Youth ministry leaders can use the *National Certification Standards* as a lens through which to assess the breadth and depth of their own capabilities. Based on that self-assessment, youth ministry leaders can develop personal learning plans to build on their strengths and to address areas of weakness. A user-friendly self-assessment tool based on the *National Standards* can be found at *www.nfcym.org.*

Conclusion

Youth ministry leadership has undergone radical transformations through the past decades, and continues to evolve and redefine itself today. One of the extraordinary signs of the vitality of youth ministry is its capacity for new initiatives, experimentation, self-reflection, and imaginative exploration of creative responses to young people in evolving faith communities in a rapidly evolving culture.

What will the near future hold for youth ministry leaders? Probably the most significant factor in that equation is the anticipated diminishment of ordained ministers. As the number of priests decreases—in some regions precipitously—so increases the need for competent, well-formed ministers of all stripes, including youth ministers. Whereas the earliest Catholic youth ministers could often manage with little theological and ministerial education, the coming Church will require laypersons with substantial theological and ministerial expertise. Moreover, youth ministry leaders will likely be called on to shoulder more of the responsibility for the general pastoral care and leadership of the faith community. Again, broader responsibilities call for broader and deeper preparation.

Youth ministry leaders have evolved, and likely will continue to evolve, into solid professional partners in the economy of parish leadership in the early years of the twenty-first century. Their experience as ministers, as coordinators of ministry, and as animators of their faith communities may uniquely qualify them for significant leadership roles in the Church to come, particularly if that experience is accompanied by the breadth of ministry preparation suggested by the *National Certification Standards*.

Chapter Questions

1. What phases of youth ministry development do you witness in your parish or faith community?
2. Which of the three leadership roles (youth minister, coordinator, animator) are you most drawn to? Which do you find the most challenging?
3. How are you affirmed, or challenged by, the *National Certification Standards for Lay Ecclesial Ministers?*
4. As you consider the future of youth ministry leadership, what developments do you think we ought to be preparing for, individually and as a Church?

Resources for Further Study and Application

Youth Ministry

Christie, Les. *How to Recruit and Train Volunteer Youth Workers: More Kids with Less Stress.* El Cajon, CA/Grand Rapids, MI: Youth Specialties/Zondervan, 1992.

Dean, Kenda Creasy, Chap Clark, and Dave Rahn, eds. *Starting Right: Thinking Theologically About Youth Ministry.* El Cajon, CA/Grand Rapids, MI: Youth Specialties/Zondervan, 2001.

Dean, Kenda Creasy, and Ron Foster. *The Godbearing Life: The Art of Soul Tending for Youth Ministry.* Nashville, TN: Upper Room Books, 1998.

East, Thomas, Ann Marie Eckert, Dennis Kurtz, and Brian Singer-Towns. *Effective Practices for Dynamic Youth Ministry.* Winona, MN: Saint Mary's Press, 2004.

East, Thomas, Ann Marie Eckert, Leif Kehrwald, Brian Singer-Towns, and Cheryl M. Tholcke. *Total Faith™ Initiative Coordinator's Manual.* Winona, MN: Saint Mary's Press, 2004.

Fields, Doug. *Purpose Driven Youth Ministry.* Grand Rapids, MI: Zondervan, 1998.

Fields, Doug. *Your First Two Years in Youth Ministry: A Personal and Practical Guide to Starting Right.* El Cajon, CA/Grand Rapids, MI: Youth Specialties/Zondervan, 2002.

Jones, Tony. *Postmodern Youth Ministry.* El Cajon, CA/Grand Rapids, MI: Youth Specialties/Zondervan, 2001.

Martinson, Roland D. *Effective Youth Ministry: A Congregational Approach.* Minneapolis: Augsburg, 1988.

McCarty, Robert J. *Thriving in Youth Ministry.* Winona, MN: Saint Mary's Press, 2005.

Mercadante, Frank. *Growing Teen Disciples: Strategies for Really Effective Youth Ministry.* Winona, MN: Saint Mary's Press, 2002.

National Federation for Catholic Youth Ministry (NFCYM). *Youth Ministry in Rural and Small Town Settings: A Planning Resource.* Washington, DC: NFCYM, 1998.

Olsen, Ginny, Diane Elliot, and Mike Work. *Youth Ministry Management Tools.* El Cajon, CA/Grand Rapids, MI: Youth Specialties/ Zondervan, 2001.

Reynolds, Sean. *Multiply the Ministry: A Practical Guide for Grassroots Ministry Empowerment.* Winona, MN: Saint Mary's Press, 1999.

Roehlkepartain, Eugene C., and Margaret R. Hinchey. *Youth Ministry That Makes a Difference.* Minneapolis: Search Institute, 1997.

United States Conference of Catholic Bishops (USCCB). *Follow the Way of Love.* Washington, DC: USCCB, Inc., 1999.

_____. *Putting Children and Families First: A Challenge for Our Church, Nation, and World.* Washington, DC: USCCB, Inc., 1999.

_____. *Renewing the Vision: A Framework for Catholic Youth Ministry.* Washington, DC: USCCB, Inc., 1997.

Adolescent Development

Barna, George. *Real Teens: A Contemporary Snapshot of Youth Culture.* Ventura, CA: Regal Books, 2001.

Howe, Neil, and William Strauss. *Millennials Rising: The Next Great Generation,* London: Vintage Books/Random House, 2000.

Kipke, Michel D. *Adolescent Development and the Biology of Puberty: Summary of a Workshop on New Research.* National Research Council, Institute of Medicine. Washington, DC: National Academy Press, 1999.

Strauch, Barbara. *The Primal Teen: What the New Discoveries About the Teenage Brain Tell Us About Our Kids.* New York: Doubleday, 2003.

Campus Ministry

Hallahan, Sr. Angela, CHF. *Doing Great Campus Ministry: A Guide for Catholic High Schools.* Notre Dame, IN: Ave Maria Press, 2003.

Nanko, Carmen. *Campus Ministry: Identity, Mission, and Practice.* Washington, DC: National Catholic Educational Association, 1997.

Wermert, Br. Dennis, SC. *Connecting on Campus: Designing and Sustaining Effective High School Campus Ministry.* Washington, DC: National Catholic Educational Association, 2004.

Catechesis

Brown, Therese, Laurie Delgatto, Christine Schmertz Navarro, and Mary Shrader. *Total Catechesis: Catechetical Sessions on Liturgy and the Sacraments*. Winona, MN: Saint Mary's Press, 2004.

Carotta, Michael. *Sometimes We Dance, Sometimes We Wrestle: Embracing the Spiritual Growth of Adolescents*. Orlando, FL: Harcourt Religion Publishers, 2002.

Congregation for the Clergy. *General Directory for Catechesis*. Washington, DC: USCCB, Inc., 1997.

Delgatto, Laurie, and Mary Shrader. *Total Catechesis: Catechetical Sessions on Christian Prayer*. Winona, MN: Saint Mary's Press, 2004.

Hagarty, Maura Thompson, Michael J. Hagarty, Marilyn Kielbasa, and Barbara A. Murray. *Total Catechesis: Catechetical Sessions on the Creed*. Winona, MN: Saint Mary's Press, 2004.

Huebsch, Bill. *Whole Community Catechesis in Plain English*. Mystic, CT: Twenty-Third Publications, 2002.

Libreria Editrice Vaticana. *Catechism of the Catholic Church*, 1st ed. Washington, DC: USCCB, Inc., 1994.

National Federation for Catholic Youth Ministry. *The Challenge of Adolescent Catechesis: Maturing in Faith*. Washington, DC: NFCYM, 1986.

Rolheiser, Ronald. *The Holy Longing: The Search for a Christian Spirituality*. New York: Doubleday, 1999.

Strommen, Merton P., and Richard A. Hardel. *Passing On the Faith: A Radical New Model for Youth and Family Ministry*. Winona, MN: Saint Mary's Press, 2000.

Tholcke, Cheryl M., with Eileen M. Daily and Steven C. McGlaun. *Total Catechesis: Catechetical Sessions on Christian Morality*. Winona, MN: Saint Mary's Press, 2004.

United States Catholic Conference of Bishops. *Our Hearts Were Burning Within Us*. Washington, DC: USCCB, Inc., 1999.

Westerhoff, John. *Will Our Children Have Faith?* rev. ed. New York: Morehouse, 2000.

White, Joseph D. *Seven Secrets of Successful Catechists*. Huntington, IN: Our Sunday Visitor Publishing Division, 2002.

Community

Eckert, Ann Marie. *Total Youth Ministry: Ministry Resources for Community Life*. Winona, MN: Saint Mary's Press, 2004.

Sofield, Loughlan, Rosine Hammett, and Carroll Juliano. *Building Community: Christian, Caring, Vital*. Notre Dame, IN: Ave Maria Press, 1998.

Evangelization

Blum, Susan. *Text, Study Guide, and Implementation Process for Go and Make Disciples*: *A National Plan and Strategy for Catholic Evangelization in the United States*. South Holland, IL: National Council of Catholic Evangelization, 1993.

Cervantes, Carmen María, ed. *Evangelization of Hispanic Young People*. Prophets of Hope, vol. 2. Winona, MN: Saint Mary's Press, 1995.

Garlinski, Michelle, Mariette Martineau, and Dean Woodbeck. *Total Youth Ministry: Ministry Resources for Evangelization*. Winona, MN: Saint Mary's Press, 2004.

Mercadante, Frank. *Make It Real! A Practical Resource for Teen-Friendly Evangelization*. Winona, MN: Saint Mary's Press, 2004.

National Federation for Catholic Youth Ministry. *The Challenge of Catholic Youth Evangelization: Called to Be Witnesses and Storytellers*. Washington, DC: NFCYM, 1993.

Family Ministry

Benson, Peter L., et al. *What Kids Need to Succeed: Proven, Practical Ways to Raise Good Kids*. Minneapolis: Free Spirit Publishing, 1998.

Chesto, Kathleen. *Exploring the New Family: Parents and Their Young Adults in Transition*. Winona, MN: Saint Mary's Press, 2001.

Kehrwald, Leif. *Parents and Schools in Partnership: A Message for Parents on Nurturing Faith in Teens*. Winona, MN: Saint Mary's Press, 2002.

Kehrwald, Leif. *Youth Ministry and Parents*. Winona, MN: Saint Mary's Press, 2004.

McGrath, Tom. *Raising Faith-Filled Kids: Ordinary Opportunities to Nurture Spirituality at Home*. Chicago: Loyola Press, 2000.

Pedersen, Mary Jo, et al. *More Than Meets the Eye: Finding God in the Creases and Folds of Family Life.* Winona, MN: Saint Mary's Press, 2000.

Rosengren, John. *Meeting Christ in Teens: Startling Moments of Grace.* Winona, MN: Saint Mary's Press, 2002.

Leadership

Calderone-Stewart, Lisa-Marie. *Changing Lives: Transformational Ministry and Today's Teens.* Dayton, OH: Pflaum Publishing Group, 2004.

Cladis, George. *Leading the Team-Based Church.* San Francisco: Jossey-Bass, 1999.

Covey, Stephen. *Principle-Centered Leadership.* New York: Fireside Books/Simon and Schuster, 1990.

De Pree, Max. *Leading Without Power: Finding Hope in Serving Community.* San Francisco: Jossey-Bass, 1997.

Eckert, Ann Marie, with Maria Sánchez-Keane. *Total Youth Ministry: Ministry Resources for Youth Leadership Development.* Winona, MN: Saint Mary's Press, 2004.

Greenleaf, Robert. *Seeker and Servant: Reflections on Religious Leadership.* San Francisco: Jossey-Bass, 1996.

Hunter, James C. *The Servant: A Simple Story About the True Essence of Leadership.* New York: Prima Publishing. 1998.

Kouzes, James, and Barry Posner. *The Leadership Challenge: How to Keep Getting Extraordinary Things Done in Organizations.* San Francisco: Jossey-Bass, 1995.

Manz, Charles. *The Leadership Wisdom of Jesus: Practical Lessons for Today.* San Francisco: Berrett-Koehler, 1998.

Sofield, Loughlan, and Donald Kuhn. *The Collaborative Leader.* Notre Dame, IN: Ave Maria Press, 1995.

Wilkes, C. Gene. *Jesus on Leadership: Discovering the Secrets of Servant Leadership from the Life of Christ.* Wheaton, IL: Tyndale, 1998.

Multicultural Ministry

Goizueta, Roberto S. *Caminemos con Jesús: Toward a Hispanic/Latino Theology of Accompaniment.* Maryknoll, NY: Orbis Books, 1995.

Perry, Theresa, and James Fraser, eds. *Freedom's Plow: Teaching in the Multicultural Classroom.* New York: Routledge, 1993.

Roberts, Elizabeth, and Elias Amidon, eds. *Life Prayers from Around the World: 365 Prayers, Blessings, and Affirmations to Celebrate the Human Journey.* San Francisco: HarperCollins, 1996.

Wilkerson, Barbara, ed. *Multicultural Religious Education.* Birmingham, AL: Religious Education Press, 1997.

www.larcheusa.org. Web site for L'Arche USA, an international network of communities devoted to affirming the dignity of and living in community with those with developmental disabilities.

Pastoral Care

Kielbasa, Marilyn. *Total Youth Ministry: Ministry Resources for Pastoral Care.* Winona, MN: Saint Mary's Press, 2004.

McCarty, Robert J. *Teen to Teen: Responding to Peers in Crisis.* Winona, MN: Saint Mary's Press, 1996.

McGlone, Gerard, Mary Shrader, and Laurie Delgatto. *Creating Safe and Sacred Places: Identifying, Preventing, and Healing Sexual Abuse.* Winona, MN: Saint Mary's Press, 2003.

National Federation for Catholic Youth Ministry. *Dealing with the Death of a Young Person: A Practical and Compassionate Response.* Washington, DC: NFCYM, 2001.

_____. *Protecting Our Young People: A Sacred Trust.* Washington, DC: NFCYM, 2002.

Roehlkepartain, Eugene C. *Building Assets in Congregations: A Guide for Youth Workers and Their Allies.* Minneapolis: Search Institute, 1997.

Roehlkepartain, Jolene L. *Building Assets Together: 135 Group Activities for Helping Youth Succeed.* Minneapolis: Search Institute, 1997.

Rowatt, G. Wade, Jr. *Adolescents in Crisis: A Guidebook for Parents, Teachers, Ministers, and Counselors.* Louisville, KY: Westminster/John Knox Press, 2001.

Prayer and Worship

Alonso, Tony, Laurie Delgatto, and Robert Feduccia. *As Morning Breaks and Evening Sets: Prayer Services for Ordinary and Extraordinary Events in the Lives of Young People.* Winona, MN: Saint Mary's Press, 2004.

East, Thomas. *Total Youth Ministry: Ministry Resources for Prayer and Worship.* Winona, MN: Saint Mary's Press, 2004.

Fleming, Austin. *Preparing for Liturgy: A Theology and Spirituality,* rev. ed. Chicago: Liturgy Training Publications, 1997.

Francis, Mark R. *Shape a Circle Ever Wider: Liturgical Inculturation in the United States.* Foreword by Anscar J. Chupungco. Chicago: Liturgy Training Publications, 2000.

Haas, David. *Music and the Mass: A Practical Guide for Ministers of Music.* Chicago: Liturgy Training Publications, 1998.

Huck, Gabe, and Gerald T. Chinchar. *Liturgy with Style and Grace,* rev. ed. Chicago: Liturgy Training Publications, 1998.

Huebsch, Bill. *A New Look at Prayer: Searching for Bliss.* Mystic, CT: Twenty-Third Publications, 1991.

Hughes, Kathleen. "Lay Presiding: The Art of Leading Prayer," in *American Essays in Liturgy.* Collegeville, MN: Liturgical Press, 1988.

National Federation for Catholic Youth Ministry. *From Age to Age: The Challenge of Worship with Adolescents.* Washington, DC: NFCYM, 1997.

Singer-Towns, Brian, et al. *Vibrant Worship with Youth: Keys for Implementing "From Age to Age: The Challenge of Worship with Adolescents."* Winona, MN: Saint Mary's Press, 2000.

Service and Justice

Bright, Thomas J., et al. *Total Youth Ministry: Ministry Resources for Justice and Service.* Winona, MN: Saint Mary's Press, 2004.

John Paul II. *On the 100th Anniversary of Rerum Novarum (Centesimus Annus). www.vatican.va.*

———. *On Social Concern (Sollicitudo Rei Socialis). www.vatican.va.*

United States Conference of Catholic Bishops. *Faithful Citizenship: A Catholic Call to Political Responsibility.* Washington, DC: USCCB, Inc., 2003.

———. *In All Things Charity: A Pastoral Challenge for the New Millennium.* Washington, DC: USCCB, Inc., 1999.

———. *A Place at the Table: A Catholic Recommitment to Overcome Poverty and to Respect the Dignity of All God's Children.* Washington, DC: USCCB, Inc., 2002.

———. *Principles, Prophecy, and a Pastoral Response: An Overview of Modern Catholic Social Teaching,* rev. ed. Washington, DC: USCCB, Inc., 2001.

———. *Sharing Catholic Social Teaching: Challenges and Directions.* Washington, DC: USCCB, Inc., 1998.

Vatican Council II. *Constitution on the Church in the Modern World (Gaudium et Spes),* in *The Documents of Vatican II.* Walter M. Abbot, gen. ed., Rev. Joseph Gallagher, trans. ed. New York: America Press, 1966.

About the Authors

General Editor

Robert J. McCarty, DMin, has worked in professional youth ministry at the parish, community, diocesan, and national levels since 1973. Bob teaches undergraduate and graduate courses in youth ministry in several colleges and presents training and formation programs on ministry issues and skills internationally.

Bob currently serves as the executive director of the National Federation for Catholic Youth Ministry, which provides resources, leadership, and vision for the development of youth ministry in the Catholic Church. He is also a parish youth ministry volunteer at Saint Francis of Assisi Church in Fulton, Maryland. Bob is the author of numerous books, including *Thriving in Youth Ministry* and *Teen to Teen: Responding to Peers in Crisis*, both published by Saint Mary's Press.

Contributing Authors

Laurie Delgatto, MA, has worked in the field of youth ministry for more than two decades, having served in parish and diocesan ministry in Texas, California, and Alabama. She has been involved in various local, regional, and national youth ministry training programs and conferences.

Laurie served as project coordinator and general editor of the Total Faith Initiative™ and is the primary author of *Church Women: Probing History with Girls* and a contributing author of *Creating Safe and Sacred Places: Identifying, Preventing, and Healing Sexual Abuse* and *As Morning Breaks and Evening Sets: Liturgical Prayer Services for Ordinary and Extraordinary Events in the Lives of Young People* (all published by Saint Mary's Press).

Rev. Tom Dunne, SDB, PhD, has been active in many forms of Catholic youth ministry and education for his forty-three years as a Salesian of Saint John Bosco. He coordinated the religious education and youth ministry programs of the Salesian Eastern Province (USA) for fifteen years. He was adjunct professor of pastoral ministry, Graduate Theological Union, Dominican School of Philosophy and Theology, Berkeley, California, from 1998 to 2001. Fr. Dunne was awarded a doctorate degree in religious education in 1989. He is presently serving as the chair of the National Federation for Catholic Youth Ministry board of directors.

Michelle Hernandez, BA, MPS candidate, is a campus minister and catechist at Immaculata High School in Marrero, Louisiana. She holds a BA in religious studies and secondary education and is currently pursuing a master of pastoral studies degree. Michelle has a passion for working with youth and for social justice, as she has served as mission club moderator for a number of years and is the service project coordinator.

Jeffrey Kaster, MA, DMin candidate, directs the Youth in Theology and Ministry program and teaches theology at Saint John's School of Theology in Collegeville, Minnesota. He completed an MA in theology (Scripture) in 1985 and is a doctoral candidate in education, policy, and administration. He is the editor of *Parish Faith Formation Assessment and Planning Tool* (Lanham, MD: Rowman and Littlefield Publishers, 1999).

Leif Kehrwald, MA, has worked in family ministry and faith formation on the parish, diocesan, and national levels for over twenty-five years. He has taught courses on family ministry, parish partnership, and family spirituality at Loyola University, Chicago; the University of Dayton, Dayton, Ohio; and Mount Angel Seminary in Oregon. Leif has written several books and numerous articles on family life, family ministry, marriage, and youth ministry. His latest book is *Youth Ministry and Parents: Secrets for a Successful Partnership* (Saint Mary's Press, 2004). A former development editor with Saint Mary's Press, Leif now serves as a project coordinator for Family and Intergenerational Ministry Services at the Center for Ministry Development.

Maggie McCarty, DMin, is the President of EPS (Education for Parish Service), a theological school for the laity at Trinity University in Washington, DC. She has been involved in youth ministry training and formation since 1977 and has experience on the parish, diocesan and national levels. Maggie serves as adjunct facility at Loyola University in New Orleans, St. Mary's Seminary and University in Baltimore, and Princeton's Institute for Youth Ministry. She is a youth ministry volunteer at St. Francis of Assisi Parish in Fulton, MD.

Frank Mercadante, MPS, is the founder and executive director of Cultivation Ministries. Since 1991 Frank has trained thousands of youth ministry leaders across the United States and internationally. He has written numerous youth ministry resources, including *Growing Teen Disciples*, *Positively Dangerous*, and *Make It Real*, all published by Saint Mary's Press.

Greg "Dobie" Moser, MA, serves as the executive director of Youth and Young Adult Ministry and CYO in Cleveland. He has an extensive background in ministering with and to youth, young adults, and families, and holds an MA in pastoral family systems counseling. He has served as the board chair for the National Federation of Catholic Youth Ministry and for the National Center for Catholic Youth Sports. Dobie has presented keynote addresses, workshops, and retreats in more than forty states and over eighty dioceses and has authored numerous catechetical and youth ministry publications.

Barbara A. Murray, MA, has been involved with the young Church in regional and national ministry, having spent fifteen years in parish and diocesan ministry in the Diocese of Lexington, Kentucky. She is the editor of *Pope John Paul II, We Love You: World Youth Day Reflections, 1984–2005* and a contributing author of *The Catholic Faith Handbook for Youth* (both from Saint Mary's Press).

Randy Raus, BA, serves as the LIFE TEEN President and CEO, helping parishes worldwide start and maintain the LIFE TEEN model of youth ministry. He has been involved in youth ministry since 1987. Randy travels extensively conducting workshops on youth ministry and is responsible for organizing a variety of conferences and youth rallies.

Sean Reynolds, MA, is the director of the Office of Youth and Young Adult Ministry of the Archdiocese of Cincinnati. Sean holds degrees in theology and organizational development. Formerly a member of the USCCB Commission on Certification and Accreditation and the chair of the NFCYM Commission on Certification and Accreditation, he was a major contributor to the NFCYM competency-based standards for the coordinator of youth ministry and the development of *National Certification Standards for Lay Ecclesial Ministers.* He is the author of many articles and resources, including *Multiply the Ministry: A Practical Guide to Grassroots Ministry Empowerment* (Saint Mary's Press, 2001). Sean has been training and mentoring youth ministers for more than twenty-five years.

Tony Tamberino, has been active in parish and diocesan youth ministry for thirty years. He is currently ministering in the archdiocese of Baltimore. Tony has also taught religious studies and theology at the secondary, undergraduate, and graduate levels and has been a contributing author for several other youth ministry resources.

Terri Telepak, MA, has worked in the field of adolescent development for twenty-five years. She has a degree in catechesis and a pontifical diploma in ministry from the Notre Dame Center for Catechetics and Ministry, granted under the auspices of the Holy See in Rome. Terri served as director of youth and young-adult ministry for the Diocese of Greensburg, Pennsylvania, for seventeen years and currently serves as pastoral associate at Saint Raphael's Parish in Bay Village, Ohio. She is a national and international speaker and frequent presenter at major ministerial conferences. Her published works include numerous articles on catechesis and youth ministry. Terri served nine years on the United States Conference of Catholic Bishops' committee on catechesis as the representative voice for Catholic adolescents. Terri presently serves on the National Catholic Adolescent Catechesis Initiative as a delegate for the NFCYM.

Anne-Marie Yu-Phelps, MEd, is director of diversity and teaches religion and Spanish at Newton Country Day School of the Sacred Heart, in Newton, Massachusetts. She also serves on the network of Sacred Heart Schools social-justice committee. She is currently pursuing a certificate of advanced educational specialization from the Institute of Religious Education and Pastoral Ministry at Boston College. Anne-Marie's previous service and justice work includes working with Vietnamese refugees in Hong Kong and Latin American refugees on the United States–Mexico border, vaccinating animals against rabies in rural Ecuador, and working in an orphan home in rural Honduras. She has also been a presenter for the Saint Mary's Press workshop "Peace, Justice, and Service in the Catholic High School."

Acknowledgments

The scriptural quotations contained herein are from the New Revised Standard Version of the Bible, Catholic Edition. Copyright © 1993 and 1989 by the Division of Christian Education of the National Council of the Churches of Christ in the United States of America. All rights reserved.

The quotation and excerpt on pages 11 and 12 are from *Hope for the Decade: A Look at the Issues Facing Catholic Youth Ministry,* by the National Catholic Youth Organization (CYO) Federation (Washington, DC: United States Conference of Catholic Bishops, Inc. (USCCB), 1980), pages 4 and 2. Copyright © 1980 by the National CYO Federation.

The material in this book labeled *Renewing the Vision* is from *Renewing the Vision: A Framework for Catholic Youth Ministry*, by the United States Conference of Catholic Bishops (USCCB) Department of Education (Washington: USCCB, Inc., 1997). Copyright © 1997 by the USCCB, Inc. All rights reserved. Used with permission.

The excerpt by John Macquarrie on page 19 is from *Principles of Christian Theology*, second edition, by John Macquarrie (New York: Charles Scribner's Son, 1977), page 1. Copyright © 1966, 1977 by John Macquarrie.

The quotations on pages 19, 21, and 134 are from *A Vision of Youth Ministry,* by the USCCB Department of Education (Washington, DC: USCCB, Inc., 1986), pages 3, 4, and 10, respectively. Copyright © 1986 by the USCCB, Inc.

The excerpts on page 21 are from *Creative Ministry,* by Henri J. M. Nouwen (New York: Doubleday, 1971), pages 111 and 116. Copyright © 1971 by Henri J. M. Nouwen.

The excerpt and quotations on pages 22, 58, and 162 are from the English translation of the *Catechism of the Catholic Church* for use in the United States of America *(CCC)*, numbers 752, 4, 2743, 2744, 2745, and 2650, respectively. Copyright © 1994 by the United States Catholic Conference, Inc.—Libreria Editrice Vaticana. Used with permission.

The quotation and excerpt on pages 23 and 195 are from *The Challenge of Adolescent Catechesis: Maturing in Faith,* by the National Federation for Catholic Youth Ministry (NFCYM) (Washington, DC: NFCYM, 1986), pages 9 and 3. Copyright © 1986 by the NFCYM.

The excerpts and quotation on pages 23, 24, and 106 are from *The Challenge of Catholic Youth Evangelization: Called to Be Witnesses and Storytellers,* by the NFCYM. (Washington, DC: NFCYM, 1993), pages 7, 20, and 3, respectively. Copyright © 1993 by the NFCYM, Inc.

The excerpt on page 30 is from "Homily for World Youth Day 1995's Prayer Vigil," number 17, by Pope John Paul II, at Eternal Word Television Network, *www.ewtn.com/library/PAPALDOC/ JP2WY10A.htm,* accessed December 15, 2004.

The excerpt on page 35 is from *I Came That They Might Have Life,* by the USCCB (Washington, DC: USCCB, Inc., 1994), page 201. Copyright © 1994 by the USCCB, Inc.

The chart on page 42 and the bulleted list of characteristics on page 43 are from *Millennials Rising: The Next Great Generation,* by Neil Howe and William Strauss (New York: Random House, 2000), pages 15 and 43–44. Copyright © 2000 by Neil Howe and William Strauss. Used with permission of Vintage Books, a division of Random House, Inc.

The statistical information for the chart on page 42 and the bulleted lists on pages 42–43 are from *Real Teens,* by George Barna (Ventura, CA: Regal Books, 2001), pages 12, 17, and 23, respectively. Copyright © 2001 by George Barna. Used with permission.

The bulleted lists on page 45 are based on *Postmodern Youth Ministry: Exploring Cultural Shift, Cultivating Authentic Community, Creating Holistic Connections,* by Tony Jones (Grand Rapids, MI: Zondervan, 2001), pages 30–37. Copyright © 2001 by Youth Specialties.

The research and statistical information listed below is from the *National Study of Youth and Religion* reports by Christian Smith and Robert Faris (Chapel Hill, NC: University of North Carolina at Chapel Hill) as follows: "Constructive v. At-Risk Behaviors" on page 48 is adapted from "Religion and American Adolescent Delinquency, Risk Behaviors, and Constructive Social Activities," report number 1, pages 7-8, copyright © 2002 by National Study of Youth and Religion; "Positive v. Negative Attitudes About Life" on pages 48-49 is adapted from "Religion and the Life Attitudes and Self-Images of

ton, NY: Edwin Mellen Press, 1982), pages 83–84, 141–142, and 3, respectively. Copyright © 1982 by the Edwin Mellen Press.

The outline of *A Single Shard* on pages 59–60 is adapted from *A Single Shard,* by Linda Sue Park (New York: Scholastic, 2001). Copyright © 2001 by Linda Sue Park. Used with permission.

The excerpt on page 61 is from *A Church to Believe In: Discipleship and the Dynamics of Freedom,* by Avery Dulles (New York: Crossroad, 1982), page 70. Copyright © 1982 by Avery Dulles, SJ.

The excerpt on page 62 and the bulleted list on pages 63–64 are from *Way to Live Leader's Guide: Ideas for Growing in Christian Practices with Teens,* edited by Dorothy C. Bass and Don C. Richter (Nashville, TN: Upper Room Books[R], 2002), pages 10 and 10–11. Copyright © 2002 by Dorothy C. Bass and Don C. Richter. Also see *www.waytolive.org.*

The bulleted list on pages 78–79 is adapted from "Ideas for Simple and Not So Simple Advocacy Strategies," in the Child Care Law Center's journal *Working for Change,* September 1995.

The bulleted lists on pages 92 and 93 are from "Effective Youth Ministry Practices in Catholic Parishes," a research project sponsored by the Center for Ministry Development and Saint Mary's Press, in collaboration with the NFCYM, pages 6 and 6. Copyright © 2003 by the Center for Ministry Development and Saint Mary's Press. All rights reserved.

The excerpt on page 93 is from *Message of the Holy Father to the Youth of the World on the Occasion of the XII World Youth Day,* numbers 4–5, at *www.vatican.va/holy_father/john_paul_ii/messages/youth/documents/hf_jp-ii_mes_15081996_xii-world-youth-day_en.html,* accessed December 15, 2004.

The excerpt on page 97 is from *Total Youth Ministry: Ministry Resources for Community Life,* by Ann Marie Eckert (Winona, MN: Saint Mary's Press, 2004), page 23. Copyright © 2004 by Saint Mary's Press. All rights reserved.

The quotation on page 106 is from *Text, Study Guide, and Implementation Process for "Go and Make Disciples": A National Plan and Strategy for Catholic Evangelization in the United States,* by the National Council of Catholic Bishops (NCCB) (South Holland, IL: National Council of Catholic Evangelization [NCCE], 1993), page 12. Copyright © 1993 by the NCCE.

bers 58, 60, 10, 12, 69, and 39, respectively. Copyright © 1997 by the NFCYM.

The excerpt from the Eucharistic Prayer for Reconciliation, II, on page 166 is from the *Sacramentary,* English translation prepared by the International Commission on English in the Liturgy (ICEL) (New York: Catholic Book Publishing Company, 1985), page 1132. English translation copyright © 1973 by the ICEL, Inc. All rights reserved. Used with permission.

The quotations on pages 167, and 168 are from *Constitution on the Sacred Liturgy "Sacrosanctum Concilium" Solemnly Promulgated by His Holiness,* numbers 14, 37, and 7, respectively, at *www. vatican.va/archive/hist_councils/ii_vatican_council/documents/vat-ii_ const_19631204_sacrosanctum-concilium_en.html,* accessed December 15, 2004.

The sections "A Christian Vision of Family Life" and "Families and Faith" on pages 173–176 and 176–178 are paraphrased from *Youth Ministry and Parents: Secrets for a Successful Partnership,* by Leif Kehrwald (Winona, MN: Saint Mary's Press, 2004), pages 126–130 and 55–56. Copyright © 2004 by Saint Mary's Press. All rights reserved.

The quotation from Pope Leo XIII on page 174 is from "Family Orphaned by the Church," by Mitch Finley, in *National Catholic Reporter,* February 28, 1986, pages 11–12.

The quotation about the Christian family on page 174 is from *Sacraments and Sacramentality,* by Bernard Cooke (Mystic, CT: Twenty-Third Publications, 1983), page 92. Copyright © 1983 by Bernard Cooke.

The quotations from Pope John Paul II on pages 174 and 183–184 are from *Apostolic Exhortation "Familiaris Consortio" of Pope John Paul II to the Episcopate to the Clergy and to the Faithful of the Whole Catholic Church on the Role of the Christian Family in the Modern World,* numbers 49, 50, 50, and 65, respectively, at *www.vatican. va/holy_father/john_paul_ii/apost_exhortations/documents/hf_ jp-ii_exh_19811122_familiaris-consortio_en.html,* accessed December 15, 2004.

The excerpts from the U.S. Catholic Bishops on pages 174 and 175 are from *Follow the Way of Love: A Pastoral Message of the U.S. Catholic Bishops to Families,* by the NCCB (Washington, DC: NCCB, 1993), page 8. Copyright © 1997 by Our Sunday Visitor Publishing Division, Our Sunday Visitor, Inc.

The quotations by Mitch and Kathy Finley on page 175 are from their *Building Christian Families* (Allen, TX: Thomas Moore, 1996), pages 18 and 16. Copyright © 1984, 1996 by Mitch and Kathy Finley.

The excerpt on page 176 is from *The Search for Common Ground: What Unites and Divides Catholic Americans,* by James D. Davidson et al. (Huntington, IN: Our Sunday Visitor Publishing Division, 1997), pages 98–99. Copyright © 1997 by Our Sunday Visitor Publishing Division.

The bulleted items summarizing key formative experiences on page 177 are adapted from "Building Strong Families Fact Sheet: A Preliminary Study" from *YMCA/Search Institute on What Parents Need to Succeed,* by Eugene Roehlkepartain, Peter Scales, PhD, Jolene L. Roehlkepartain, Carmelita Gallo, and Stacey P. Rude. Copyright © 2002 by YMCA of the USA and Search Institute^{SM,} at *www.abundantassets.org/building.cfm,* accessed December 15, 2004. All rights reserved. For more information visit *www.abundantassets.org.*

The U. S. Census Bureau statistics on page 179 are from "America's Families and Living Arrangements, March 2000," at *www.census. gov/population/socdemo/hh-fam/p20-537/2000/tabF1.txt,* accessed December 15, 2004.

The statistics on children in single-parent homes on page 179 are from "American Association for Single People," at *www.singles rights.com/main.html,* accessed December 15, 2004.

The information on mothers who are employed outside the home on page 179 is from the FamilyEducation.com Web site, at *familyeducation.com/home,* accessed December 15, 2004.

The excerpt on page 184 is from "Pastoral Visit in Australia, *Homily of John Paul II,* Perth, Australia, November 30, 1986," number 3, at *www.vatican.va/holy_father/john_paul_ii/homilies/1986/documents/ hf_jp-ii_hom_19861130_perth-australia_en.html,* accessed December 15, 2004.

The quotation and excerpt by Virgilio Elizondo on pages 189 and 189–190 are from *Multicultural Religious Education*, edited by Barbara Wilkerson (Birmingham, AL: Religious Education Press, 1997), pages 397–398 and 397. Copyright © 1997 by Religious Education Press.

The excerpt about the bishops' statement on page 193 is from *Always Our Children: A Pastoral Message to Parents of Homosexual*

Children and Suggestions for Pastoral Ministers, at *www.usccb.org/ laity/always.htm,* accessed December 15, 2004. Copyright © 1997 by the USCCB, Inc.

The excerpt on pages 218–219 is from *The Godbearing Life: The Art of Soul Tending for Youth Ministry,* by Kenda Creasy Dean and Ron Foster (Nashville, TN: Upper Room Books, 1998), page 30. Copyright © 1998 by Kenda Creasy Dean and Ron Foster.

The bulleted summary lists of the National Certification Standards on pages 233–234 are adapted from *National Certification Standards for Lay Ecclesial Ministers,* by the National Association for Lay Ministry (NALM), the National Conference for Catechetical Leadership (NCCL), and the National Federation for Catholic Youth Ministry (NFCYM) (Washington, DC: NALM, NCCL, NFCYM, 2003), pages 1–11, respectively. Copyright © 2003 by the NALM, NCCL, and NFCYM.

To view copyright terms and conditions for Internet materials cited here, log on to the home pages for the referenced Web sites.

During this book's preparation, all citations, facts, figures, names, addresses, telephone numbers, Internet URLs, and other pieces of information cited within were verified for accuracy. The authors and Saint Mary's Press staff have made every attempt to reference current and valid sources, but we cannot guarantee the content of any source, and we are not responsible for any changes that may have occurred since our verification. If you find an error in, or have a question or concern about, any of the information or sources listed within, please contact Saint Mary's Press.

Endnotes Cited in Quotations
from Documents Copyrighted by the USCCB

1. National Catechetical Directory NCCB. 1976, 176d.
2. Cf. John Paul II, apostolic exhortation, *Catechesi tradendae* 1; 2.
3. AG 14.
4. Cf. AG 13; EN 10; RM 46; VS 66; RCIA 10.
5. EN 14.
6. EN 20; cf. EN 63; RM 52.
7. DCG (1971) 19d.
8. Cf. DCG (1971), 21.
9. *"Declaration of the Synod Fathers,"* 4: L'Osservatore Romano (27 October 1974), p. 6.
10. 1 *Pt* 3:15.
11. *Dei Verbum* 8.
12. See *CCC* #1069–1090.
13. At the Youth and Worship Summit meeting in October 1994, one participant described the goal as a "full court press" of dialogue and action among local leaders to respond to the challenges of involving youth in worship.
14. See *CCC* #1074-1075; 2688.
15. Sr. Thea Bowman, FSPA, adapted the phrase "It Takes a Whole Church" from the Ghanian proverb "It takes a village to raise a child."